THE PICKLEBALL BIBLE

STUDENT EDITION

With Assignments and Performance Score Sheets

By Dr. Rick B. Lambson & Tim Finger
With Robert Thompson

PUREPickleball

Rules & Play
Serve
Ground Strokes
Drop Shot
Volleys
Overheads
Lobs
Strategies
Drills
Mental Game
Illustrations
Assessments

About the Authors

Dr. Rick B. Lambson

Rick is married to Kat Lambson and is the proud father of 3 exceptional daughters: Sara Suzanne, Lauren Leigh, and Mia Danielle. Dr. Lambson is a physical educator/exercise scientist and athletic coach who has taught and coached students in elementary through university graduate programs. Rick graduated with a doctorate degree in exercise science from Brigham Young University and has served as the Physical Education and Human Performance Department Chairman for over 10 years and Head Women's Tennis Coach at Southern Utah University in Cedar City, Utah.

Rick has coached a variety of sport teams including: baseball, basketball, football, golf, tennis, swimming, track & field, and volleyball. He also actively participates in sports such as golf, swimming, racquetball, tennis, and pickleball. In the past 15 years Dr. Lambson has won over 120 medals in 20 different events in state, regional, and open competition and was the first player to win a singles gold medal in pickleball during the Utah Summer Games.

After being honored in California as Wilbur Jr. High School and Cubberley High School Athlete of the Year, Rick played baseball as a collegiate scholarship athlete, earning the Scholar Athlete Award as a sophomore. Later in his career he won two National USTA Team Tennis Championships with his Amarillo, Texas Team.

Rick loves to teach and has been recognized with several teaching awards including SUU Professor of the Year.

Tim Finger

Tim Finger is married to Connie and has 2 beautiful daughters, Stephine and Christina. Tim (BS Weber State University) is a highly sought after personal tennis and pickleball consultant. He discovered his interest in a variety of sports at a young age and began playing tennis at age 8. Rising quickly through the ranks of competitors, Tim faced off and held his own against other amateurs and pros like Matt Mitchell (NCAA Champion), Nick Saviano (quarter-finalist at Wimbledon) and Brad Gilbert (top 10 ranked player in the world). He was the top player on his Weber State tennis team during the 1978 and 1979 seasons before turning Pro at the age of 24. His passion for the sport eventually led to him to develop a comprehensive teaching style that not only teaches the skills of the game, but also combines academics and nutrition into his training.

Tim made the transition to pickleball quickly, becoming the top nationally ranked player in 2008 in his division. Using his coaching skills and knowledge of racquet sports, he quickly began applying his comprehensive teaching and training style to this new sport. He now has over 100 young and older clients that he instructs on a regular basis.

Interested in the sport expanded in 2010 when he decided to get into the retail business by manufacturing and selling balls and paddles. In 2010 his company entered into a retail selling relationship with both Dicks Sporting Goods and Big5. Tim has expanded his pickleball business venture to include quality educational and manufactured equipment and other products.

Acknowledgments

> "I just want to thank everyone who made this day necessary." –Yogi Berra (Hall of Fame catcher for the NY Yankees)

We give our thanks and appreciation to all those who encouraged and supported this effort, especially to our families. The original Tres Amigos (Rick, Tim and Robert), also express appreciation to the fabulous four (Joey Brown, Eric Pedersen, Jacob Pedersen and Erik Bylund), who have now joined the Pickleball Magic and PurePickleball teams. It takes a community to raise a great organization and develop great pickleball players.

Published by PurePickleball, Inc.
St. George, Utah, USA
Website: www.purepickleball.com

And Starry Night Publishing,
Rochester, NY.

Register your book at www.purepickleball.com for free video updates on drills, skills, and strategies, and receive the next edition free.

***For the paperback copy, be sure to buy The Pickleball Bible DVD to view all 60 referenced videos.**

Contents

Introduction 9

The Game 9

The Court 12

Equipment 12

Paddles 12

Balls 13

Nets and Posts 13

Basic Rules 13

1. **Scoring** 13

2. **Serve** 13

3. **Serving Sequence Singles** 13

4. **Serving Sequence for Doubles** 13

5. **Double Bounce Rule** 13

6. **Non-Volley Zone** 14

7. **Line Calls** 14

Etiquette/Sportsmanship 14

Basic Grip 15

SKILL NO.1 SERVE 157

Skill Strategy: The Quiet Eye Technique 18

Skill Strategy: Basic Serve Routine 18

BOWLING BALL OR BASIC SERVE 18

BACKHAND SERVE 24

THE RUNNING SERVE 26

SPIN SERVES 27

LOB SERVE 28

Skill Strategy: Serve Consistency 31

Student Assignment No 1.1: 32

Student Assignment No. 1.2: 32

PICKLEBALL Serve - PERFORMANCE SCORE SHEET 32

SKILL NO. 2 RETURN OF SERVE/GROUND STROKES 33

Skill Strategy: Basic Return of Serve 34

Skill Strategy: Basic Return of Serve and Ground Strokes 35

Student Assignment No. 2.1: Determine your DOMINANT EYE 35
Cues & Errors: Return of Serve and Ground Strokes 36
Skill Strategy: Adjustment Steps 38
Return of Serve/Ground Strokes Drills: 39
Student Assignment No. 2.2: 40
Student Assignment No. 2.3: 40
GROUND STROKE - PERFORMANCE SCORE SHEET 40
SKILL NO. 3 LONG DROP SHOT 41
Cues & Errors: Long Drop Shot 41
Student Assignment No. 3.1 42
LONG DROP SHOT - PERFORMANCE SCORE SHEET 42
Skill No. 4 Dink 43
Cues & Errors: Dinking in Doubles 43
Skill Strategy: Partners in Sync 43
Dink Drills 44
Student Assignment No. 4.1 45
DINK SHOT - PERFORMANCE SCORE SHEET 45
ADVANCED KITCHEN SHOTS FOR DOUBLES 46
1. The Cobra 46
2. The Hallway or The Avenue 46
3. Lob off the dink 47
Dink to Lob Drill Video 47
SKILL NO. 5 VOLLEYS 48
5.1 BASIC VOLLEY 48
Skill Strategy: Paddle Position 49
5.1 Basic Volley Drills 49
5.2 SOFT BACKSPIN OR DROP VOLLEY (Advanced Technique) 49
5.3 APPROACH SHOT TO VOLLEY 50
5.3 Cues & Errors: Approach Shot to Volley 51
5.4 LOW VOLLEY 52
5.4 Cues & Errors: Low Volley 52
5.5 BACKHAND SWEEP 53
5.5 Cues & Errors: Backhand Sweep 53
Student Assignment No. 5.1 54
Student Assignment No. 5.2 54

VOLLEY - PERFORMANCE SCORE SHEET 54
SKILL NO. 6 HALF-VOLLEY 55
Cues & Errors - Half-Volley 55
Skill Strategy: Split Stop 55
Half-Volley Drill 58
Student Assignment 6.1: 59
HALF-VOLLEY - PERFORMANCE SCORE SHEET 59
SKILL NO. 7 OVERHEAD SMASH 60
Cues & Errors - Overhead Smash 60
Skill Strategy: Returning a Lob 62
Skill Strategy: Return of Smash 62
Smash Drill 63
Student Assignment 7.1 64
OVERHEAD SMASH - PERFORMANCE SCORE SHEET 64
SKILL NO. 8 LOB 65
Skill Strategy: Lob 65
An offensive lob 65
Return of lob 65
Cues & Errors - Lob 66
Lob Drill 67
Student Assignment 8.1: 68
LOB - PERFORMANCE SCORE SHEET 68
BOOK III: MORE DRILLS, GAMES AND ACTIVITIES 69
PRACTICE & COMBINATION DRILLS 69
1. Serve, Return, Drop Drill (Doubles) 69
2. Lob, Smash, Return (Singles or Doubles) 69
LEAD-UP GAMES 70
1. Half-Court Singles 70
2. The Kitchen Game 70
3. Modified Games 70
BOOK IV: GAME STRATEGIES 71
Skill Strategy: Keep the ball in Play 71
Skill Strategy: If it works… 71
SINGLES 71
1. SERVE 71

2. RETURN OF SERVE & GROUND STROKES 71
3. COURT POSITIONS 72
4. NET PLAY 72
5. GENERAL CONSIDERATIONS 73
DOUBLES 74
1. SERVING TEAM 74
2. RETURNING TEAM 75
3. GENERAL COURT STRATEGIES 75
4. COMMUNICATION 77
BOOK V: MENTAL PREPARATION 78
1. MENTAL PRACTICE AND IMAGERY 78
1.1 MENTAL PRACTICE 78
1.2 INTERNAL & EXTERNAL PERSPECTIVES 79
1.3 NOVICE AND HIGH PERFORMANCE ATHLETES 79
1.4 PAIVIO'S CONCEPTUAL MODEL OF IMAGERY 79
PAIVIO'S CONCEPTUAL MODEL OF IMAGERY 79
7 PRINCIPLES AND APLLICATIONS OF MENTAL PRACTICE 80
2. GOAL ORIENTATION 82
2.1 TASK (MASTERY) GOAL ORIENTATION 82
2.2 EGO (COMPETITIVE) GOAL ORIENTATION 82
3. GOAL SETTING 83
3.1 BASIC TYPES OF GOALS: 83
3.2 IMPORTANT CHARACTERISTICS OF GOALS 83
PRINCIPLES AND APPLICATIONS GOAL SETTING 84
4. SELF-CONFIDENCE 85
4.1 EARLY RESEARCH BY ALBERT BANDURA 85
BANDURA'S ELEMENTS OF SELF-CONFIDENCE (Self-Efficacy) 85
4.2 CONFIDENCE VS ARROGANCE 86
5. ATTENTION/CONCENTRATION 87
5.1 DIRECTING ATTENTION 87
DIRECTING ATTENTION Principles and Applications 87
6. MENTAL TOUGHNESS 89
6.1 HOW IS MENTAL TOUGHNESS TRAINED? 89
7. CHOKING 90

7.1 SHIFTING FROM AN EXTERNAL FOCUS OF ATTENTION TO AN INTERNAL FOCUS OF ATTENTION (BAD IDEA!) 91

7.2 PARALYSIS BY ANALYSIS (ANOTHER BAD IDEA!) 91

7.3 THE IRONIC EFFECT 91

Strategies to overcome the ironic effect: 91

8. "THE ZONE" or "Unconscious Competence" 92

8.1 THE ZONE FILE 92

8.2 CHARACTERISTICS OF A PHYSICAL GENIUS 92

8.3 PERFORMANCE ROUTINES 93

FINAL WORD 94

VI. TALKING THE WALK GLOSSARY 95

BOOK I: THE BEGINNING

Introduction

In the beginning Joel gathered paddles, balls and nets and created the magic game: and saw that it was good. He divided humanity into teams: and it was so. The game brought forth fun and laughter: and Joel saw that it was good.

And the evening and the morning of the next day Joel created rules and gave the game the name pickleball and thereafter named his dog Pickles. And Joel said let the game bring forth players of all ages that they might have joy: and it was so.

And Joel blessed the players and said unto them have fun, be fruitful and have dominion over all other games. And Joel saw everything that he had created: and behold it was very good.

And on the next day Joel rested from all his labors and played the magic game.

Joel Pritchard

The Game

Sometime between 1963 and 1966 on Bainbridge Island, Washington, Joel Pritchard and his friend Bill Bell using only ping pong paddles, an old badminton court, a net, and a whiffle ball invented a game to involve the whole family. The game now known as "Pickleball" (A name probably derived from row boats called "pickle boats" and probably not from the famous Pritchard dog named after the game.) is a fast paced game that involves hand-eye coordination skills that are used in many racket sports such as tennis, ping pong, paddleball, and racquetball. For a more complete history Ctrl Click the following links: Pickleball History or check out "A Doggone Name?"

One of the most amazing characteristics of pickleball is that it can be played by anyone at any age at any level, making it an ideal family activity. During the past 5 decades pickleball has flourished and has become one of America's favorite participatory sports. It has been played in backyards, middle schools, high schools, has found a place in university activity curriculums, and is now becoming popular as a collegiate club sport.

Breaking News No. 1! We now have the photos of the first historical pickleball picture ever taken under ***Delicate Arch***-Arches National Park, near Moab, Utah.

Breaking News No. 2! **Santa Claus** was found playing pickleball at the Scottish Games in Moab, Utah, and has graciously consented to take orders for this book and other merchandize at this website link: **PurePickleball.com**

Photo by Rick Lambson

Skill Levels

The International Federation of Pickleball (IFP) has established 9 skill level ratings: 1.0, 1.5, 2.0, 2.5, 3.0, 3.5, 4.0, 4.5, and 5.0. There are also 3 rating types: 1. Self-Rating, 2. Appealed Rating, and 3. Tournament Rating. Most players will rate themselves based on the IFP Rating System IFP Rating Description (Ctrl click to follow link).

The IFP Rating is primarily based on stroke proficiency and a players understanding and application of rules and strategies. Age, physical disabilities and mobility should be considered when assigning a skill level. A player may have the stroke and strategy capability but is handicapped by a physical disability. In addition, few players over 50 should be rated in the 5.0 category which should reflect a high degree of athleticism as well as stroke proficiency.

Pickleball is usually played from the waist down and shoulders up. Bending at the knees and getting your tail closer to the ground will certainly improve your game. If you are having trouble getting close to the ground without lying down, leg strengthening exercises will greatly help. As an individual ages the number one factor in loss of independence is a loss of leg strength. Big biceps are esthetically nice, but leg strength is absolutely essential not only for pickleball but for a high quality of life. We can't forget the mental aspect. Check out *Book V* for some awesome mental preparation techniques.

The Court

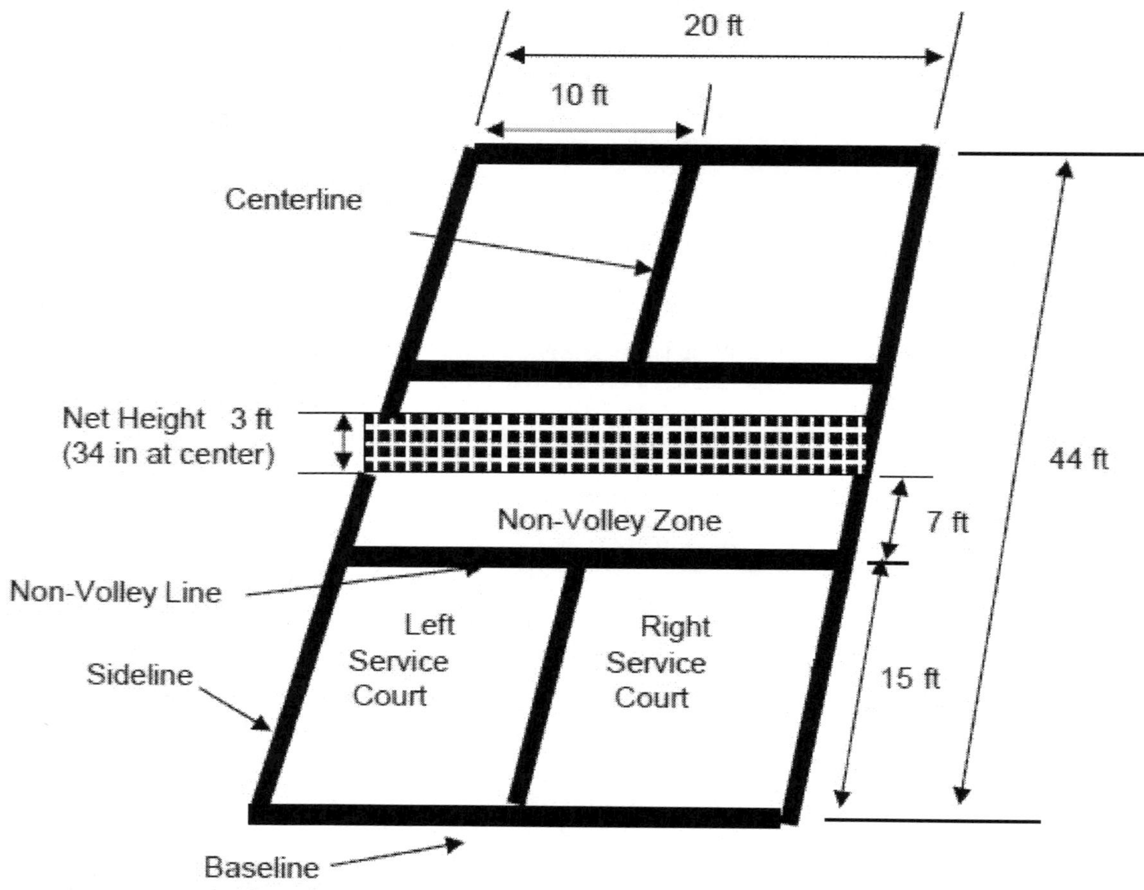

Additional information on court dimensions specifications and construction guidelines can be found here Court Information (Ctrl Click)

Equipment

Paddles: Materials: Paddles may be made of any relatively rigid, non-compressible material such as graphite, fiberglass, or aluminum. The hitting surface cannot contain holes, indentations, rough texturing, tape or anything that is highly reflective or that can increase the spin on the ball. (Impact deflection with a force of 3 kg may not produce a deflection greater than 5 thousandths of an inch which may produce a trampoline effect and threaten the nature of the game.)

Size: The combined length and width including any edge guard and butt cap shall not exceed 24 inches.

Weight: There is no weight restriction.

Balls: Outdoor balls usually are made of harder more durable plastic with smaller holes.

Materials: Balls shall be made of durable plastic molded with a smooth surface and free of texturing.

Size/Weight: Balls shall be 2.75 to 3.00 in diameter and weigh between 0.8 and 1.02 oz.

Tournament directors may determine the tournament ball.

The International Federation of Pickleball (IFP) has the task of judging whether paddles and balls meet specific uniform standards. For more information on paddle and ball material, size and deflection rates access the following links: 1. Paddle Specs, 2. Ball Specs.

Nets and Posts:

- Nets may be made of any open meshed fabric small enough to prevent a ball from passing through it.
- Net dimensions shall be 20 x 2.5 feet.
- Height at sidelines is 36 inches and 34 inches at center court.
- Top of net should have a two inch wide binding over cord or cable.
- Posts should be placed 1 foot outside of sidelines.

Basic Rules (Be ye therefore diligent in keeping all the rules.)

1. **Scoring:** Points are only scored when serving.
    a. Games are usually played to 11 points with the winning player or team having a 2 point advantage. Often in consolation games, the final score may be extended to 15 points at the discretion of the tournament director.
    b. When calling out the score in doubles, the server will call out his/her score, the opponents score and which server he/she is (No. 1 or No. 2).
2. **Serve:** The ball is served underhand without bouncing it, and must be contacted below the waist. The serve is made to the diagonal service court.
    a. Lines are considered "in" except for the short service line or "kitchen" line.
    b. Both feet must be behind the baseline.
    c. If the serve hits the net and otherwise is good, the serve will be replayed (service let).
    d. After the score has been called, the server and receiver has 10 seconds to be ready.
3. **Serving Sequence Singles:**
    a. At the start of each game, the server will start on the right side ("deuce" side) and will change service sides only after scoring a point.
    b. Serves will always be on the right side when the server's score is even and on the left side ("add" side) when the score is odd.
4. **Serving Sequence for Doubles:**
    a. The service always starts on the right side and changes service sides when a point is scored.
    b. The team's points will be even when the game's starting server is on the right-hand side.
    c. The team starting the game will default the serve after one fault. Thereafter, each player on each team will be allowed to serve until they lose their serve.
5. **Double Bounce Rule:** The receiver must let the serve bounce once before the return and the serving side must let the return bounce once. After each side hits a ground stroke, the players are then permitted to volley or hit the ball before it bounces.

6. **Non-Volley Zone:** A player cannot volley a ball while standing in the "kitchen" or non-volley zone, however a player may enter the kitchen to return a shot that has bounced in the zone.
7. **Line Calls:**
    a. It is the responsibility of the players to call the line balls on their side of the court.
    b. No player should question an opponent's call unless asked.
    c. When looking across line do not call a ball out unless you can clearly see the space between the line and the ball. "The opinion of a player looking down the line is more likely to be accurate than one looking across the line." (IFP Rulebook, 6.D.5)
    d. Calls should be made immediately.
    e. A ball is presumed "in" unless it is called "out" promptly.

For questions on rules refer to this link: Rules

Etiquette/Sportsmanship (Rejoice not when thine opponent loses.)

Sportsmanship is about respect for opponents, officials, teammates, coaches, and especially the game. Winning is fun, but relationships are what makes life worth living. Few people if any, will remember how many metals you've won, but they will remember how you treated them.

"At its best, athletic competition can hold intrinsic value for our society. It is a symbol of a great ideal: pursuing victory with honor. The love of sports is deeply embedded in our national consciousness. The values of millions of participants and spectators are directly and dramatically influenced by the values conveyed by organized sports. Thus sports are a major social force that shapes the quality and character of the American culture." – *Arizona Sports Summit Accord 1999*

"One man practicing good sportsmanship is far better than fifty others preaching it." – Knut Rockne, the legendary Notre Dame Football Coach

Basic Grip

1. Keep it simple with a "hand shake" grip. Place your palm flat on the paddle face. Then slide it down to the handle and close your fist.
2. Thumb should touch the 2nd finger NOT the index finger. The index finger should be your "trigger finger" and be located above the thumb, otherwise it is a "hammer grip" and you definitely don't want to be hammering nails with that beautiful paddle.
3. This one grip will work for almost any type of hit. It is especially useful at the kitchen where volleys come fast and furious with no time to consciously change grips.

Snap Shot: Basic Grip

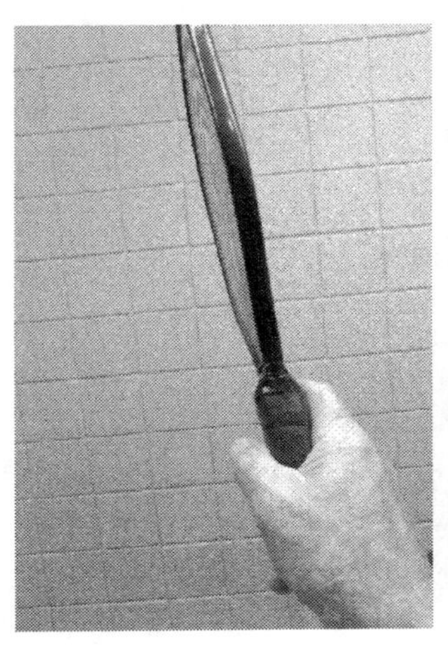

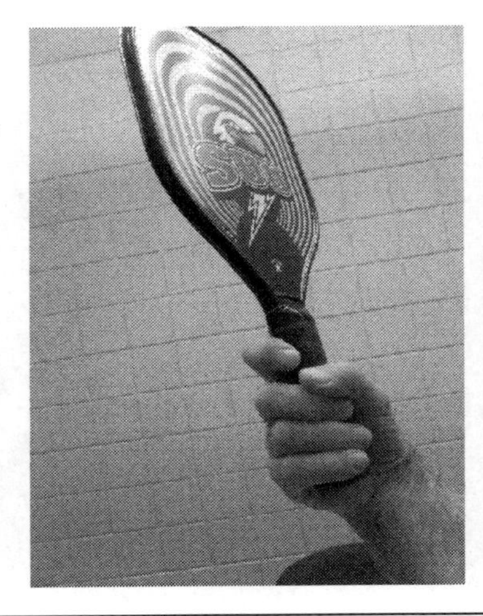

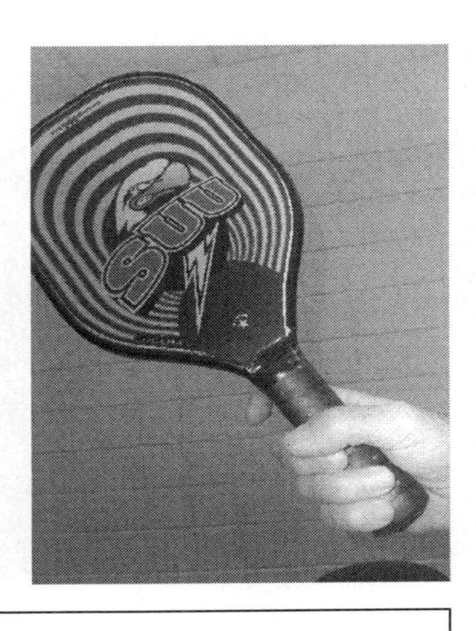

1. "V" on Top **2. Nice Trigger Finger** **3. Good Hand-shake**

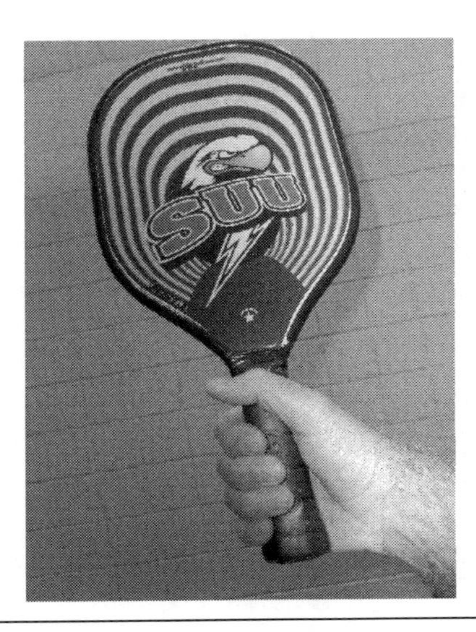

Hammer Grip – Use this grip to hammer nails not hit pickleballs!

Basic Body Position

Get in an athletic ready position:

1. Head up, shoulders square, spine straight with slight forward lean, knees slightly bent, and weight slightly shifted to balls of your feet. Do not lock the knees! Now you look like a linebacker or a runner on first base, ready to steal second base. For you "non-athletes" don't worry about the previous analogy…you look great!

Snap Shot: Ready Position

THE GOOD THE BAD & UGLY

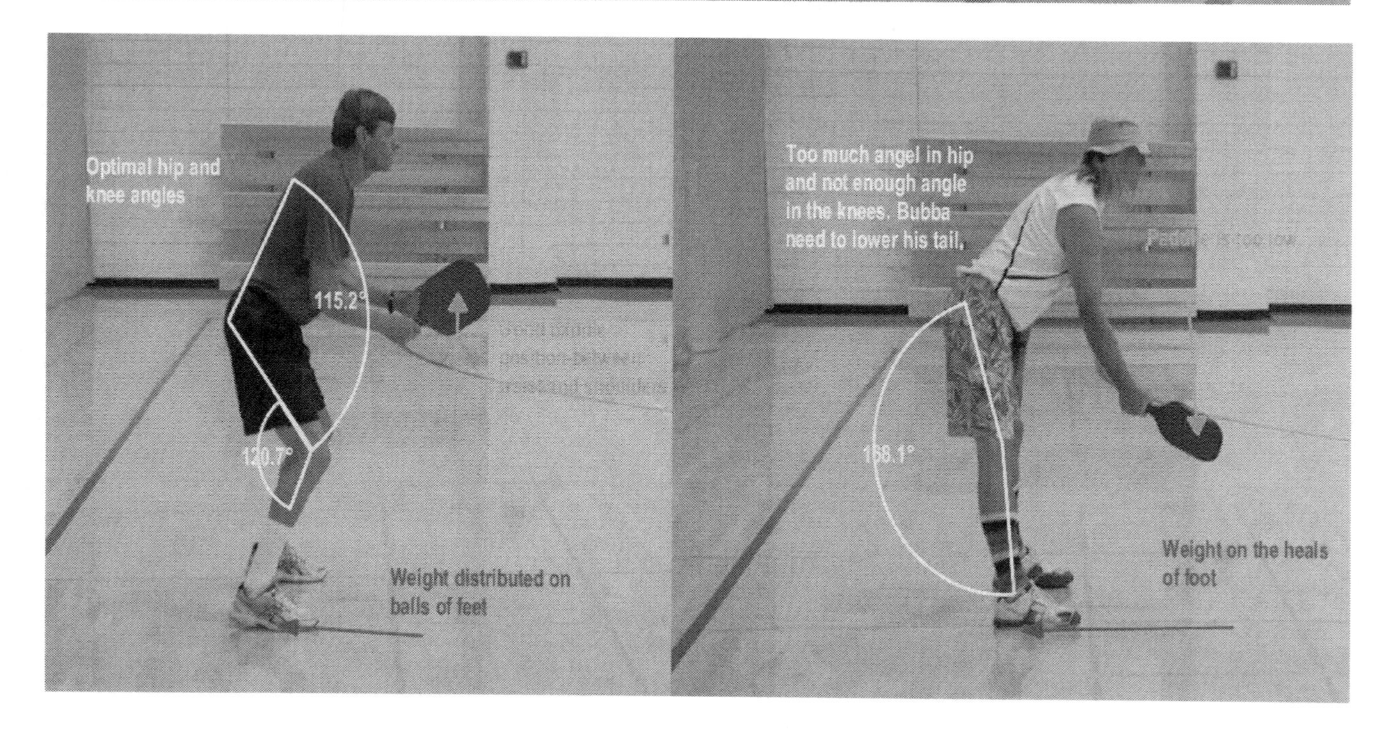

BOOK II: THE LUCKY 8 - SKILLS AND DRILLS

For the Chinese, the number 8 is considered lucky just like the number 7 is considered lucky in the West. Therefore, it should come as no surprise that the Olympic Games in China started on August 8, 2008 or 08/08/08. In China you have to pay extra to have the number 8 in your phone number or license plate. In addition, home and business owners like to have the number 8 in their address. (We didn't have to pay extra to use the number 8 in this book, and we didn't charge you extra.)

八

So, why is the number 8 considered auspicious in the minds of Chinese people? The main reason has to do with the pronunciation of the word for the number 8 in China. It is pronounced "ba" and sounds like the word for prosperity which is pronounced "fa". Another reason why the number 8 could be considered lucky is because it has a perfect symmetrical shape and is perfectly balanced. If the number 8 in half vertically or horizontally, both halves mirror themselves perfectly. Perfect symmetry lends itself to perfect balance. In the eastern cultures perfect balance is considered the ideal. As athletes we also strive for perfect balance as a means to optimal performance.

Balanced Rock-Arches National Park

SKILL NO. 1 SERVE

Overview: The second most important shot in pickleball is the deep serve. **(The first most important shot in doubles is the drop shot in the kitchen.)** All serves must be hit below the waist and out of the tossing hand. Each player should find the serve or serves that can consistently (90-100%) be placed deep in the service court. The chance of getting an ace on a serve is very slim. The main objective of the serve is to put the ball in play and increase the chances of a weak return. Once you can get a high percentage of serves in play, then you can get more aggressive by adding more speed, spin or tighter placement.

Eye hath not seen the things which we hath prepared for them that read this book.

Skill Strategy: The Quiet Eye Technique

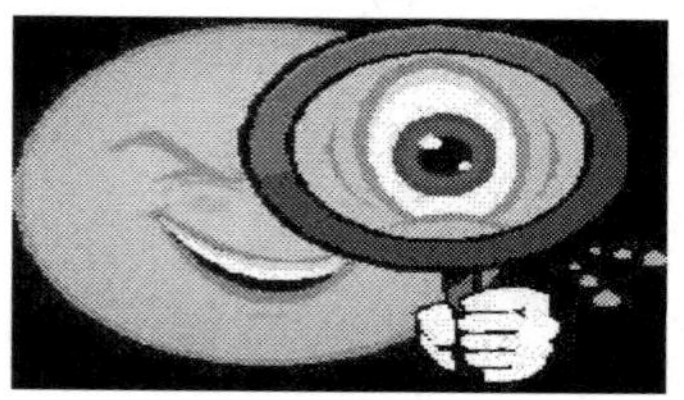

"Quiet Eye" research by J.N. Vickers discovered important differences between expert and non-expert performers when aiming at a far target. The Quiet Eye technique is a pre-execution period of visual fixation that contains a systematic routine. The expert's visual fixation period preceding shot execution was longer (1.5 to 2 seconds), the number of fixations were fewer, and fixation ceased earlier than non-experts. (Vickers, J.N. (1996) Visual Control when aiming at a far target. Journal of Experimental Psychology: Human Perception and Performance, 22, 342-354)

So what significance does this have with a pickleball serve? If you follow the "Quiet Eye" routine your percentage of legal serves with excellent placement will skyrocket.

Skill Strategy: Basic Serve Routine

1. Use the "Quiet Eye" routine for serving:
- Choose your type of serve
- Take your stance and direct focus on a specific serving target
- Maintain eye fixation for 1.5 to 2.0 seconds while saying in your mind "sight, focus"
- Change focus to the ball and serve without hesitation
2. Serve deep and to opponent's backhand or weakest side.
3. Advanced players can add variations of speed, placement and spins to disrupt opponent's concentration and force them into hitting a slightly different return

1-BOWLING BALL OR BASIC SERVE

1.1 Cues & Errors: Bowling Ball or Basic Serve

Teaching Cues:	Common Errors:
1. Handshake grip 2. Focus on target area (Quiet Eye Routine) 3. Lay the wrist back and lock it throughout the entire stroke 4. Tip of paddle pointing to the ground 5. Step to the target line 6. Turn hips, shoulders and feet toward paddle side (about 45 degrees from the net)	1. No body turn 2. Not keeping the eyes on the ball to the paddle 3. Releasing the wrist and hitting the ball too high

7. Tossing hand should be palm up (When the ball is released from the tossing hand in this manner the ball will remain longer in the hitting zone than a straight drop from the hand with the palm facing the ground. We learn this tip from world class ping pong players.) 8. Transfer weight to front leg 9. Contact with the ball should be in front of the body and just above knee height 10. Imagine hitting 3 consecutive balls toward the target 11. Keep nose pointing at the ball or in other words, keep your eye on the ball	4. **Decelerating** (Deceleration is a common killer for many sport skills…putting, basketball shooting, bowling, tennis, racquetball etc. Deceleration will change the sequence of muscle contraction and thus change the entire motor program necessary for skill movement.) 5. Not transferring weight to front leg and in direction of the target 6. Lifting chin up, which will often result in a net serve

Snap Shot: Follow-Through

Imagine hitting 3 consecutive balls in the direction of the intended target. Your weight transfer and momentum should also be directed toward the target. This mental technique works extremely well for serves, return of serves, ground strokes and most volleys.

Snap Shot: Basic Grip for all Serves (Keep it simple)

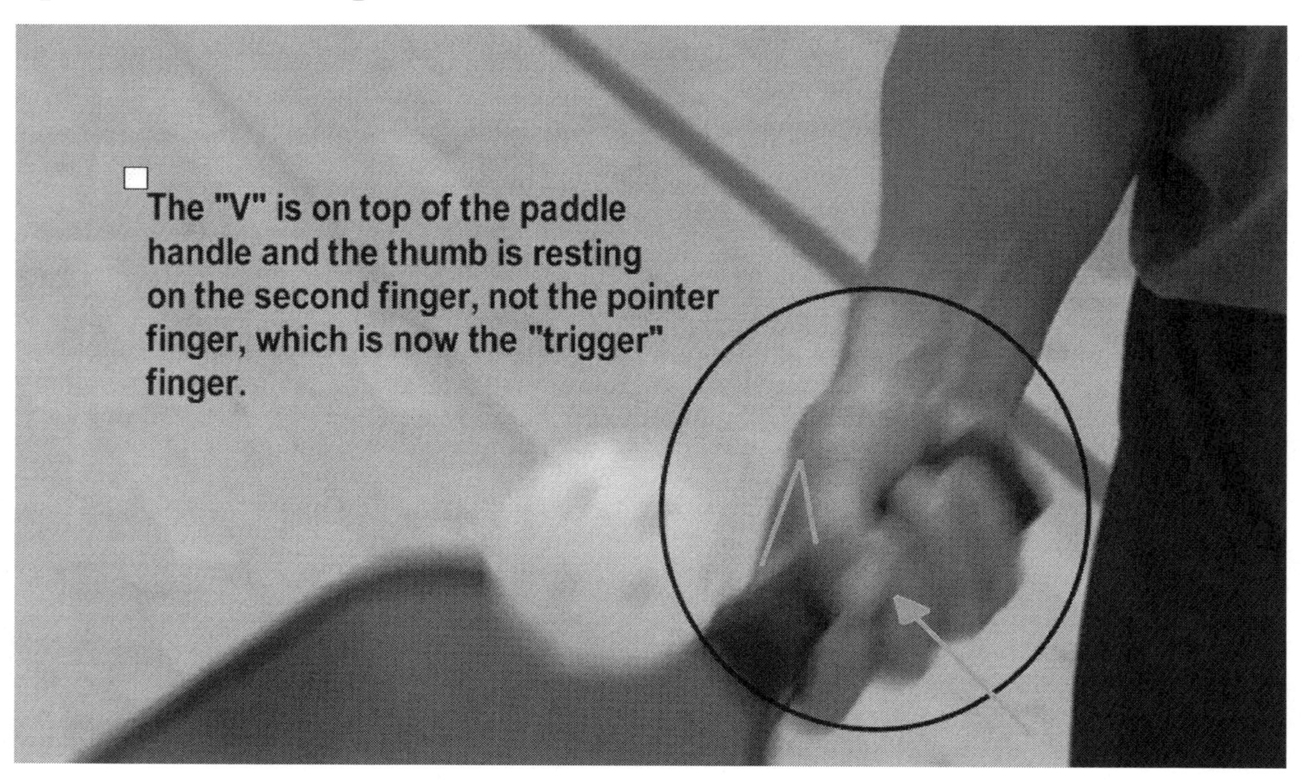

Snap Shot: Bowling Ball or Basic Serve

The Good

Contact Point

After Serve Position

Ball flight

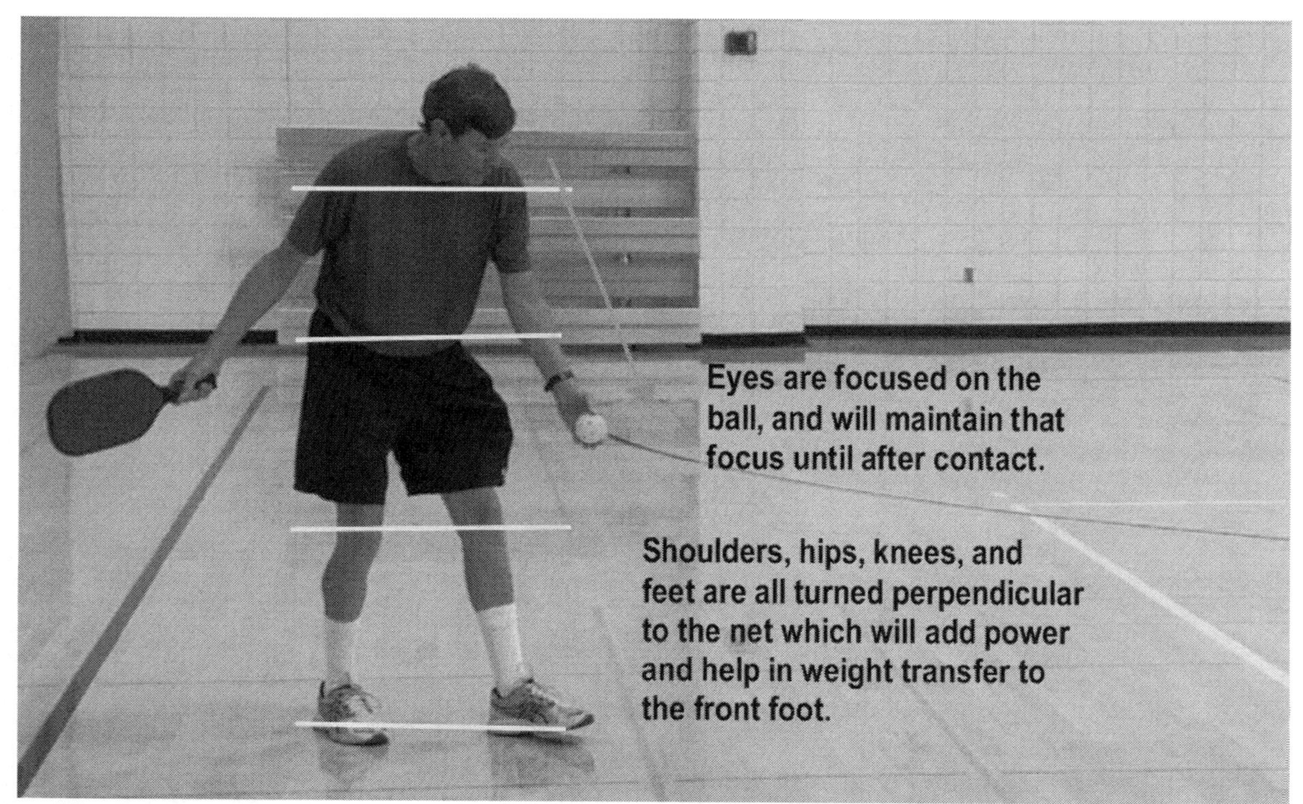

Note: The legs and hips will start the forward swing with a horizontal rotation. The faster the spin, the more power generated.

The Bad

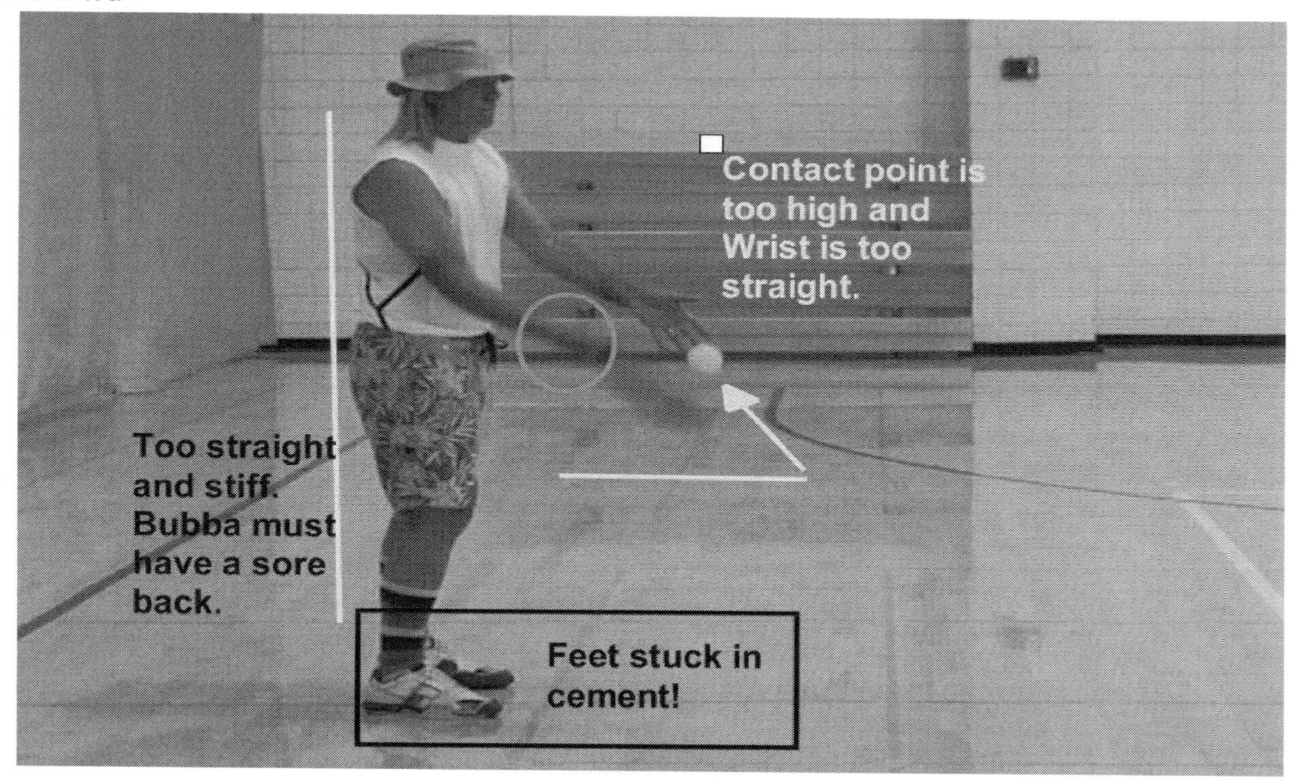

1.1 Bowling Ball or Basic Serve Videos:

Video 1.1: Basic Serve-Good vs Bad - .25 speed

Video 1.2: Basic Serve-Tim - .50 speed

Video 1.3: Basic Serve-Front View Good vs Bad - .25 speed

Video 1.4: Basic Serve-Ball Flight StroMotion - .25 speed

2-FLAT SERVE

1.2 Cues & Errors: Ground Stroke or Flat Serve

Teaching Cues:	Common Errors:
Same for the Bowling Style except for the following: 1. Tip of paddle is pointing more to the side rather than straight down 2. Contact point is at or slightly below the equator and to the outside half of the ball imparting an inside-out spin	Same for the Bowling Style except for the following: 1. Rotating the palm toward the midline or in a supinated position usually results in a short serve with an "outside-in" spin that lacks accuracy 2. Not transferring weight to front leg

Snap Shot: Flat Serve

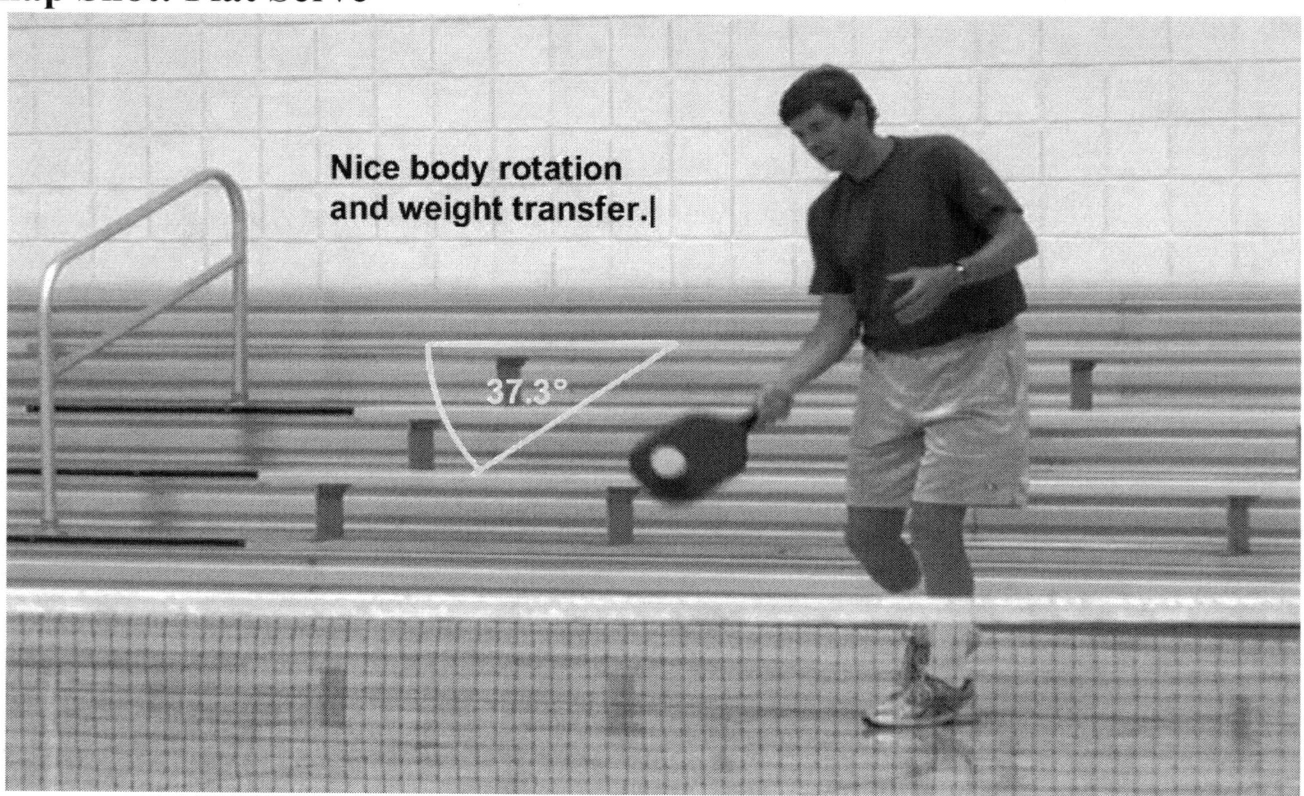

1.2 Forehand Serve Videos:

Video 1.5: Flat Serve-Front View Bad - .25 speed

Video 1.6: Flat Serve-Angle of Paddle - .25 speed

Video 1.7: Flat Serve-Birdseye View - .25 speed

3-BACKHAND SERVE

1.3 Cues & Errors: Backhand Serve

Teaching Cues:	Common Errors:
1. Rotate shoulder, hips and feet to the non-paddle side 2. Step forward with paddle side leg 3. Drop ball over the hitting arm and in front of leading leg (you may also feed the ball from underneath the hitting arm) 4. Swing toward line of target with firm wrist 5. Keep your nose pointing to the ball	1. Turning the palm too far downward or in a pronated position. This usually results in a short inside-out spin with little accuracy 2. Hitting the ball too close to the body 3. Not getting weight transferred to the front leg

Snap Shot: Backhand Serve

THE GOOD

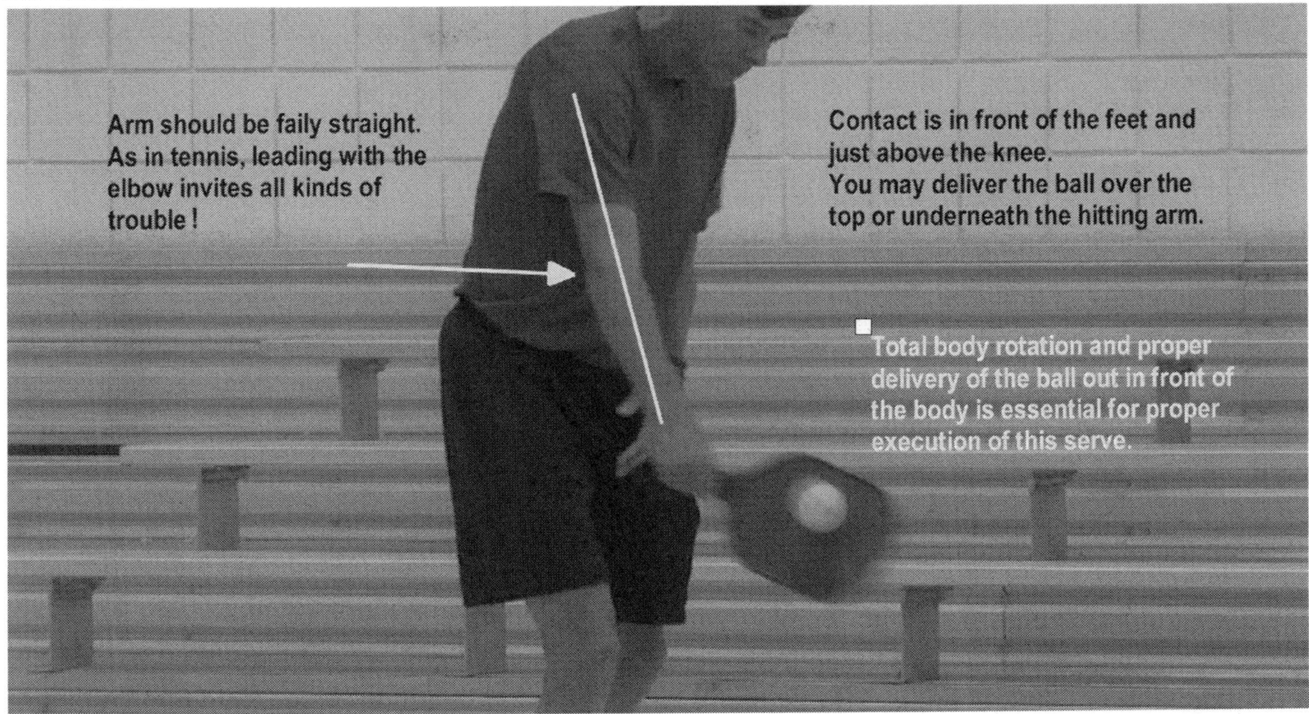

THE BAD

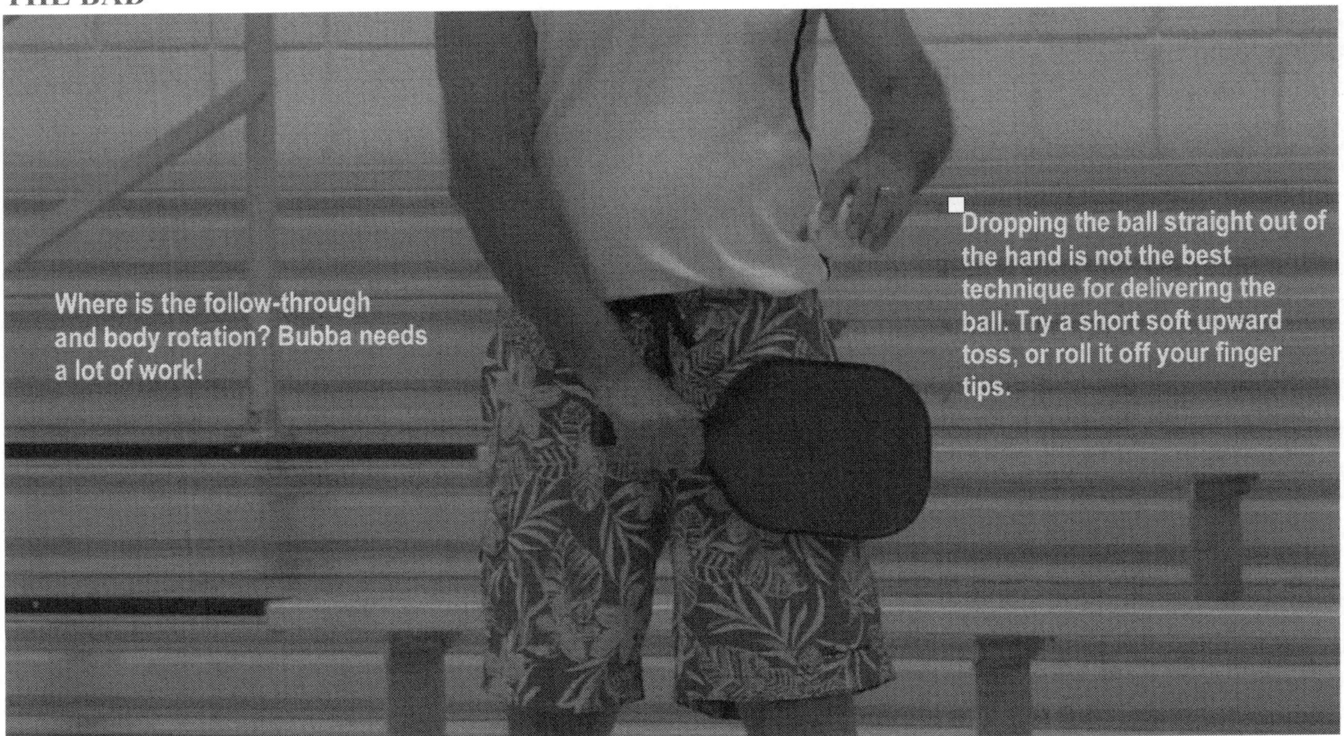

1.3 Back Hand Serve Videos:

Video 1.8: Backhand Serve Good - .25 speed

Video 1.9: Backhand Serve Bad - .25 speed

4-THE RUNNING SERVE

The running serve can be used to: 1. Increase velocity of the serve, 2. Change court position with your doubles partner, or 3. Disrupt the concentration or anticipation of your opponent.

1.4: Cues & Errors: The Running Serve

Teaching Cues:	Common Errors:
1. Before the approach use the "quiet eye" technique to focus on target, but once the approach is started, the focus must be on the ball! 2. Use a slow controlled running approach to the service line 3. The approach can be straight on, or from the side 4. Start moving arm and cocked wrist cocked back to a ready position on the first steps 5. You can hit off of either foot	1. Shifting focus to target before contact 2. Running too fast 3. Waiting too long to get the arm in a hitting position

Snap Shot: Running Serve

Snap Shot: Side Running Serve

1.4 Running Serve Videos:

Video 1.10: Running Serve - 1.0 speed

Video 1.11: Running Serve - .25 speed

Video 1.12: Side Running Serve - 1.0 speed

5-SPIN SERVES

Spin serves can be useful in pulling your opponent out of position, forcing them to hit with a weaker backhand stroke, or as a change of pace.

1.5 Cues & Errors: Spin Serves

Teaching Cues:	Common Errors:
1. Just before contact, rotate the palm of the paddle hand upward or in a supinated position 2. The paddle will make initial contact with the ball at the equator and slide southward 3. The paddle must continue forward and upward toward the target line 4. The contact point is slight higher up from the knee than the flat serves	1. Hitting too low on the ball 2. An exaggerated side to side follow through

Snap Shot: Spin Serve

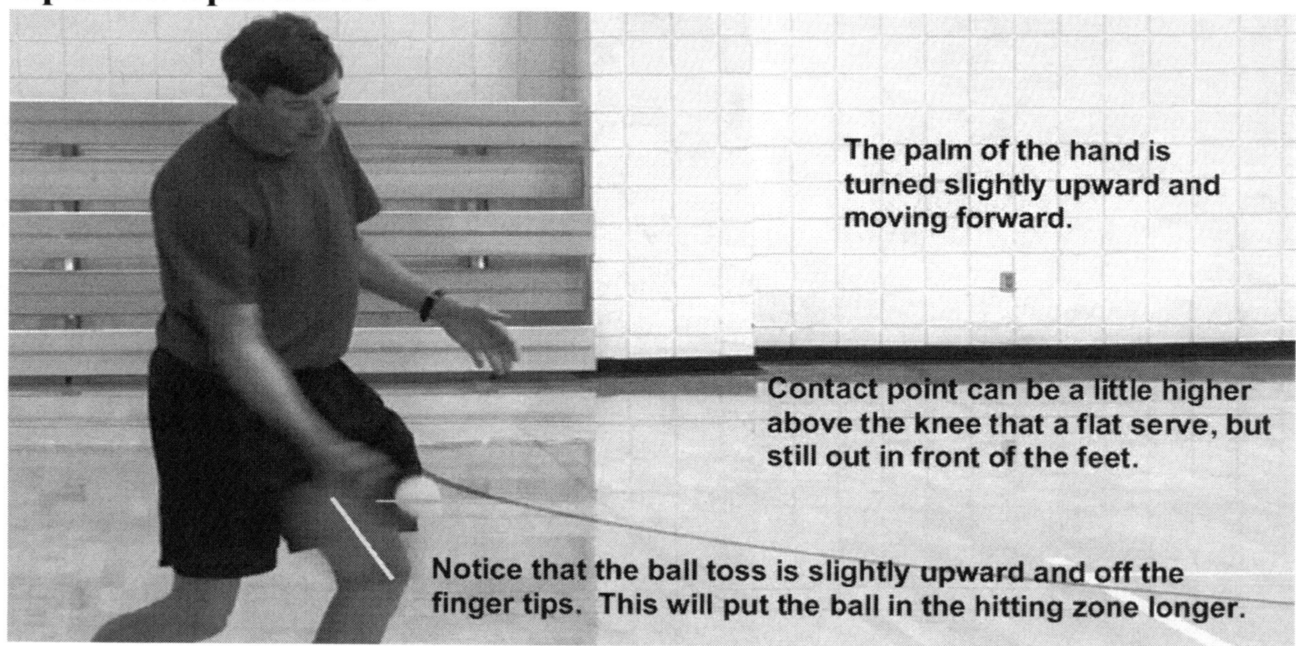

1.5 Spin Serve Videos:

Video 1.13: Spin Serve Close-up - .25 speed

Video 1.14: Spin Serve Forehand - 1.0 speed

6-LOB SERVE

Lob serves can catch an opponent off-guard and occasionally the return will sail long or wide because of the extra power your opponent tries to impart on the return hit.

1.6 Cues & Errors: Lob Serve

Teaching Cues:	Common Errors:
1. Contact the ball well below the equator 2. Bend the knees and lift with the legs 3. Follow through to at least eye level 4. Try to impart top-spin by brushing up the back side. This will help the ball stay in play 5. This serve should be deep to the baseline	1. Too short of a serve 2. No knee bend 3. No follow through

Snap Shot: Lob Serve

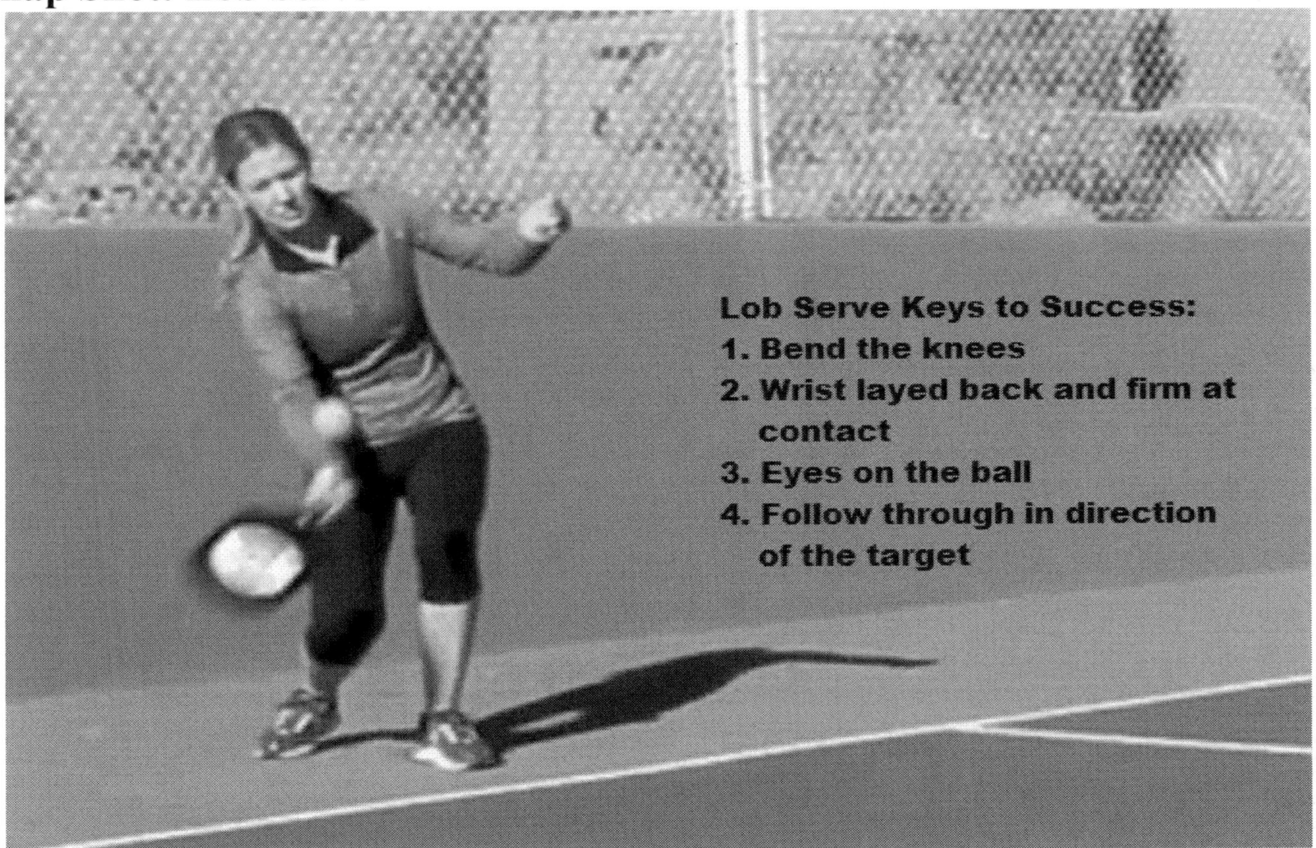

1.6 Lob Serve Video:

Video 1.15: Lob Serve - .25 speed

Video 1.16: Lob Serve - .50 speed

Snap Shot: Serving Drills

1. Serve and catch drill: This drill will show your opponent's position on the court and at what height contact will be made. Targets are always a good addition to serving drills.

2. Hit the spot drill: Similar to the serve and catch drill but you don't have to catch. You can also have your partner practice the return shot.

Serving Drill Video:

Video 1.17: Serve and Catch Drill - .25 speed

Skill Strategy: Serve Consistency

The final spin: You can serve flat, side spin, top spin, back spin, or lob, but the best serve is the one that you can get in play 90 to 100% of the time. Use your consistent serve most often but practice others. Remember to practice placement (backhand side of opponent) as well as speed and spin.

Student Assignment No 1.1: Choose 2 of the 6 serves and list what you consider to be the 5 most important cues. Write down and memorize these cues by associating each hand with one of the serves and the 5 cues for each serve with the fingers on the associated hand. These papers may be collected, and you may be asked to verbally repeat the cues by your instructor during practice or a game.

Student Assignment No. 1.2: Serve 10 times using your most consistent serve and have your classmate/partner complete a Performance Score Sheet. Hula Hoops or taped areas may be used as target areas. Groups of 3 work really well for competing the Performance Work Sheets.

PICKLEBALL Serve - PERFORMANCE SCORE SHEET –
TYPE:________________
Name:____________________ Scorer's Name:___________________ Date:_________

Skill Segment:	**Score: 0,1,2**
1. Handshake grip	
2. Focus on target area	
3. Lay the wrist back and lock it throughout the entire stroke	
4. Step toward the target line	
6. Rotate hips, shoulders and feet toward the intended target	
7. Transfer weight to front leg	
8. Contact the ball in front of the body and just above knee height.	
9. Acceleration through the ball	
10. Eye on the ball…Nose pointing to the ball	
Score (20 pts)	
Number of serves in target X 2 (20 pts)	
Total Score (40 pts)	
Scoring: 0 = Needs more practice 1= Good but needs a little more consistency 2 = Mastered	

SKILL NO. 2 RETURN OF SERVE/GROUND STROKES

Overview: **His bad shots shall return upon his own head.**

The return of serve, forehand and backhand ground strokes have many common elements because of the distance the ball has to travel and the time available for return preparation. Therefore, the common cues and common errors will be combined where applicable.

Every stroke in pickleball or any other racquet sport requires a concentrated focus on the ball. If you move your focus from the ball at any time during the stroke you will probably lose control of where the ball will go. Players have a big tendency to look at where the ball is supposed to go rather than watching the ball to contact. This concept is no more important than in the return of serve, ground strokes, volleys and overheads…in other words, every stroke in the game!

Skill Strategy: Visual Systems

There are **2 visual systems** that all athletes must understand and utilize for optimal performance.

1. The focal vision system is used primarily to identify objects in the center of the visual field and contributes to our conscious perception of objects.

2. Ambient Vision involves both the central and peripheral portions of the visual field and is specialized for movement control. It detects position, speed and direction of objects outside of focal vision and contributes to fine motor movements without our conscious awareness. Ambient vision also provides us with information about our own movements and our relative position to environmental objects. **Athletes need to appreciate and utilize the valuable information provided by the ambient vision system**.

By relying on and trusting the ambient visual system, players will feel much more confident in keeping an eye on the ball. When using the ambient vision and the "Quiet Eye" technique (See Skill Strategies:" Quiet Eye" under Skill No. 1 Serve) together, consistent ball contact and placement will be phenomenal.

Tunnel Arch-Arches National Park. Keep your eye on the ball and rely on your ambient vision system for movement and position of your opponent(s).

Skill Strategy: Basic Return of Serve

Start the "Quiet Eye" routine for return of serve.

1. **As you approach your ready position, decide what type of return is your 1st option. (Option 2 might be a medium soft deep return if you are forced to stretch for the ball and are unable to set up properly)**
   i. **Force: hard, medium, soft, lob**
   ii. **Direction: deep, short angle, backhand corner, to weak partner etc.**
   iii. **Most returns should be executed with your strongest side (forehand or backhand) even if you must "run around" the ball (As you progress to upper levels of play you may add return options according to the placement, spin and speed of the serve.)**
2. **Focus on a specific return target for 1.5-2.0 seconds and assume the ready position**
3. **Change focus to the paddle/ball area of the server**

Snap Shot: Return of Serve Placement Options

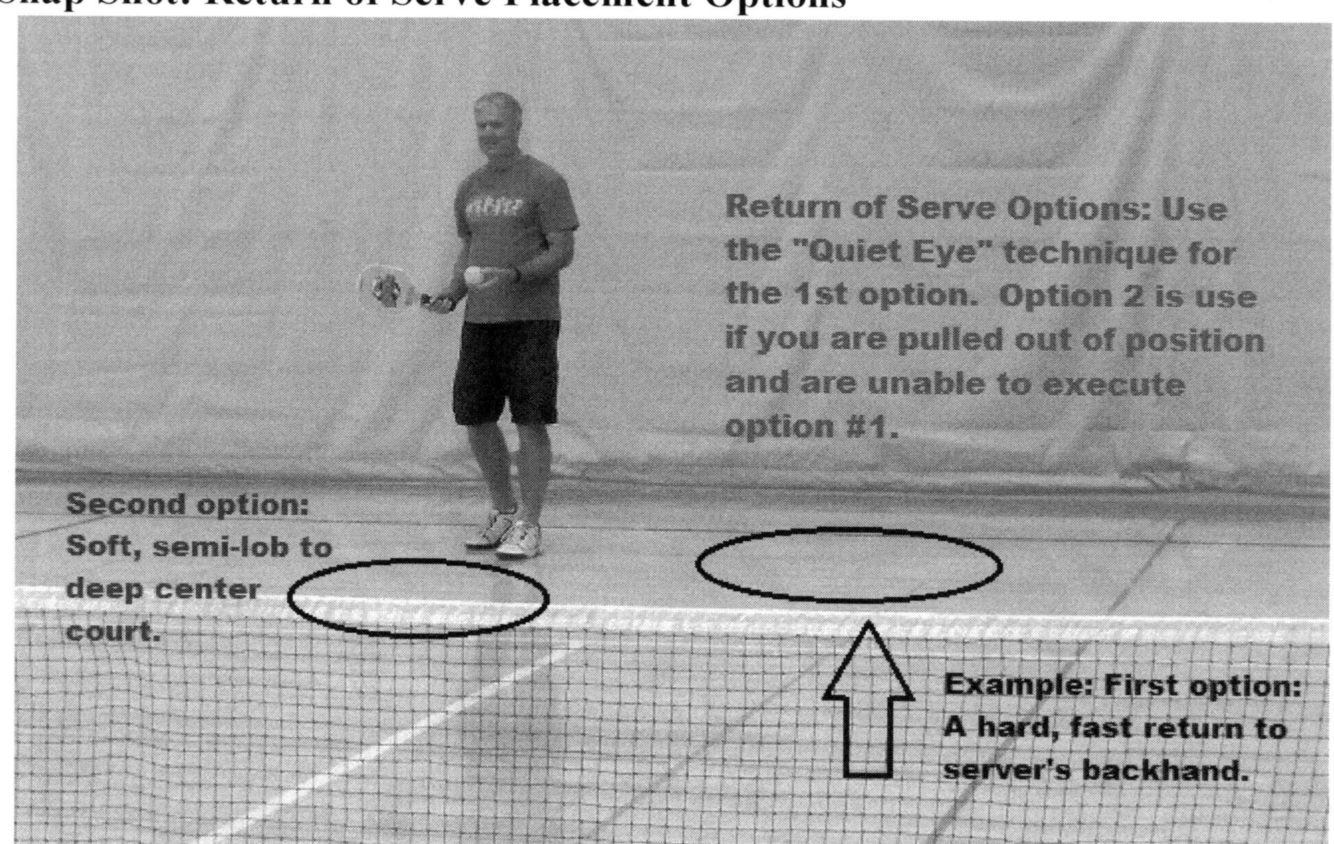

Skill Strategy: Basic Return of Serve and Ground Strokes

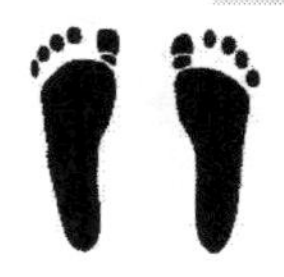

1. **Move the feet first to position body.**
   (Many beginning and some advanced players have "sleepy feet" which has a messy effect on their strokes. "Happy feet" may be the answer to improve poor stroke production. Feet position is the key to balance and balance is good!)
2. **Hips, Shoulders and early paddle preparation** will follow the feet and are essential to both backhand and forehand returns. How far do you turn? That will depend on which is your dominant eye (see "Student Assignment – Dominant Eye" below)
3. **Contact ball in front of body toward the net**

Student Assignment No. 2.1: Determine your DOMINANT EYE

Eye dominance is the visual equivalent of handedness. Each individual has a dominant eye which controls many important visual functions, such as the ability to aim, and directing focus of attention. It also guides the other eye and directs attention and fixation on moving environmental objects. This suggests that the dominant eye plays a significant role in the development of sports skills, pickleball not being an exception.

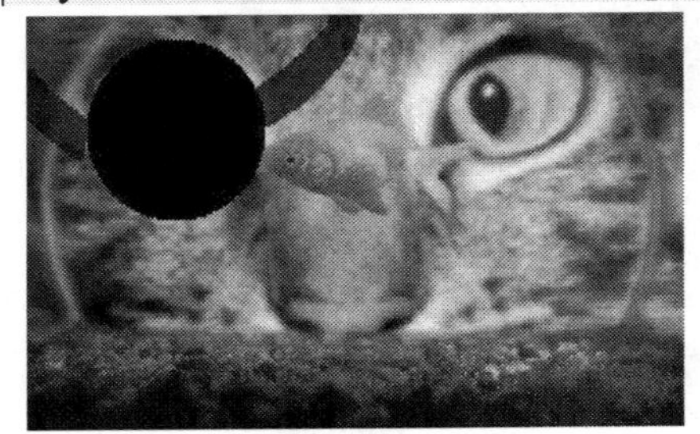

The majority of the population (85%) are PURE DEXTRALS (Right-handed, right-eye dominant or left-handed and left-eye dominant). The remaining 15% of the population are CROSS DEXTRALS (Right-handed left-eye dominant or left-handed and right-eyed dominant).

The assessment for determining the eye dominance is very easy: Extend fingers and arms with and palms facing away from the body as if pushing against a wall. Overlap the hands and create a triangular window with the thumbs and index fingers. With both eyes open, focus on a target about 20 feet away within the window. Now close your left eye. If you still see the object you are right-eye dominant and if the object moved out of sight you are left-eye dominant.

Pure dextral pickleball players, baseball players and golfers may all suffer from the same visual impairment when hitting forehand ground strokes, hitting a pitched ball or trying to line up a putt. Hitting with a closed stance or with the eyes directly over a putt most likely is less effective for pure dextrals because the bridge of the nose will partially obstruct the vision of the dominant eye which could result in loss of precision. So how far should you rotate your body on a forehand ground stroke if you are a pure dextral? How about 45 degrees as opposed to 90 degrees? However, on the backhand side a full 90 degree rotation will work just fine. If you are a cross-dextral, just the opposite will hold true.

Snap Shot: Ground Stroke Set-Up Options & Eye Dominance

A. Closed Position: "Cross Dextral"- Rt. Handed/Left Eye Dominant
B. Open Position: "Pure Dextral"- Rt. Handed/Right Eye Dominant
When hitting with either set-up position, the ball should always be contacted in front of the belly-button!

A

B

Cues & Errors: Return of Serve and Ground Strokes

Teaching Cues:	Common Errors:
1. Athletic position with knee slightly bent 2. Turn: Initiate turn by stepping with outside foot to the right or left. (If you are starting your turn with your shoulders…you have sleepy feet which is not good.) 3. Hips, shoulders, and paddle will follow the foot (How much of a turn will be determined by your eye dominance) 4. Step forward with front foot 5. Shift weight to front leg while bending knee to absorb the weight transfer (How do you know if you have proper weight transfer? If you can raise your back heel off the ground	1. Sleepy feet…get the weight on the balls of the feet 2. Reacting too slowly to direction of the ball 3. Locked knees (Too stiff) 4. Sloppy wrist 5. Looking up before contact 6. Contacting ball too late and not out in front 7. Rolling wrist over ball = in the net 8. Scooping paddle upward = soft looping return or too long (Tip of paddle is pointing toward the ground.) 9. Deceleration of the paddle through the ball

without moving your whole body forward, then you've got it!) 6. Rotate hips on contact (Belly button should be pointing toward the net if you are not late getting to the ball.) 7. If possible the paddle should be horizontal to the ground and the wrist firm 8. Eye on the ball (trust your ambient vision) 9. Contact ball in front of the waist toward the net for forehand and further out in front for the backhand ground stroke 10. Hit through the ball (Imagine hitting 3 consecutive balls just as you did in the serve.) 11. Don't admire your shot just yet…get into position for the return shot	

Snap Shot: Return of Serve Position for Fast, Hard Serves

Snap Shot: Backhand Ground Stroke

Skill Strategy: Adjustment Steps

Even under the most controlled situations (during drills etc.), the ball will not always go to the ideal hitting area, making it difficult for the student to properly transfer the weight directly into the shot. Students need to understand and implement the concept of adjustment steps. These steps are the final quick steps to get the body in correct position before the final step into the ball.

It is also very important that as player chases down a wide or short ball, the paddle should be back and in a ready position as there will be no time to initiate any back swing. When chasing down a short ball the paddle should be held lower and in a shorter backswing ready position as it is usually a low ball. The position of the paddle for a short ball should ideally remain in a horizontal position with a slight upward angle. This will require bending the knees and getting the tail low.

Anticipating where the ball will be returned is also extremely valuable for increasing quickness. This can be done by studying the body position and paddle angle of your opponent and by moving before the ball crosses to your side of the net. You snooze you lose.

Return of Serve/Ground Stroke Skill Videos:

Video 2.1: Three Ground Stroke Birdseye 1.0 speed

Video 2.2: Forehand & Backhand Ground Strokes Side 1.0 speed

Video 2.3: Open Stance Forehand Ground Stroke 1.0 speed

Return of Serve/Ground Strokes Drills:

1. Rally with Partner.
2. Controlled Rapid Return Drill (3+ balls): Feeder should vary speed and direction.
3. Multiple Ball Rally with Partner

Return of Serve/Ground Stroke Drill Video:

Video 2.4: Controlled Rapid Return Drill 1.0 speed

Student Assignment No. 2.2: Write down and memorize what you consider to be the 5 most important cues associated with ground strokes.

Student Assignment No. 2.3: After receiving 10 forehand and 10 backhand ground stroke feeds from your classmate/partner, complete a Performance Score Sheet for ground strokes. Hula Hoops or taped areas may be used as target areas.

GROUND STROKE - PERFORMANCE SCORE SHEET

Name:________________________ Scorer's Name:____________________ Date:__________

Skill Segment:	**Score: 0,1,2**
1. 1st Step "Happy Feet" (Body rotation initiated by moving feet 1st)	
2. Early paddle preparation	
3. Weight transfer to forward leg	
4. Eyes on ball	
6. Contact ball out in front	
7. Paddle tilted towards a horizontal rather than a vertical position	
8. Firm wrist	
9. Acceleration through the ball	
10. Return to ready position	
Skill Score (20 max. pts)	
Number of stokes in target (20 max. pts)	
Total Score (40 max. pts)	
Scoring: 0 = Needs more practice 1= Good but needs a little more consistency 2 = Mastered	

SKILL NO. 3 LONG DROP SHOT

Overview: The long drop shot from the baseline is considered by many the most important shot in doubles. The long drop shot should probably not be used in singles unless your opponent is lame or has fallen flat on his/her rear near the baseline. It is usually the 3rd shot of a rally. The serving team with two players back at the baseline, has a disadvantage in getting to the kitchen line because of the double bounce rule. The receiving team will already have one player at the net and with a decent return should have both players in volley position. The team that can control the volley zone first will have a distinct advantage in winning the rally.

Cues & Errors: Long Drop Shot

Teaching Cues:	Common Errors:
1. On the return, move your feet and try to get into a balanced position ready for the 3rd shot 2. Eyes on the ball 3. Weight transfer to front leg in anticipation of moving to the kitchen line 4. Swing toward line of target with firm wrist 5. Best target is usually to the player that is back or coming to the net. Dropping the ball down the middle (Sometimes referred to as the "Hallway" or "Avenue") can also be an effective shot 6. Get the ball over the net, even if it goes long 7. The non-hitting partner should take one step into the court and watch the partner's return 8. If the 3rd shot return is weak it is better that both partners stay back 9. Do it together (Never leave your partner alone…move up and back together…side to side together.) 10. Be patient (Look for a good opportunity to come to the net together.) 11. If the second shot (return) is short, an occasional hard smash down the middle might be substituted for the long drop shot	1. Not following the ball to contact (Use your ambient vision to locate position of the opposing team.) 2. Trying to hit a winner from the baseline 3. Not moving together as a unit 4. Lack of patience

Long Drop Shot Skill/Drill Video:

Video 3.1: Long Drop Shot with Drill 1.0 speed

Student Assignment No. 3.1: Standing at the baseline, you will attempt 10 long drop shots as your partner feeds you easy ground strokes. Your partner will then complete a Performance Score Sheet for the Long Drop Shot.

LONG DROP SHOT - PERFORMANCE SCORE SHEET

Name:____________________ Scorer's Name:__________________ Date:________

Skill Segment:	**Score: 0,1,2**
1. Good foot work (Balanced position)	
2. Weight transfer moving forward	
3. Eyes on ball	
4. Contact ball out in front	
6. Paddle in horizontal position	
7. Firm wrist	
8. Acceleration through the ball	
9. Good decision to go or stay back	
10. Smile on face	
Skill Score (20 max. pts)	
Number of drop shots in target x 2 (20 max. pts)	
Total Score (40 max. pts)	
Scoring: 0 = Needs more practice 1= Good but needs a little more consistency 2 = Mastered	

Skill No. 4 Dink

Overview: The dink is another very important shot in pickleball and is a 2nd cousin 3 times removed from the drop shot. The Dink is a soft shot that is initiated close to the net and lands in the kitchen area. This is one shot that needs a lot of practice but can be done at home without a partner against a solid wall with an uncarpeted floor. If you have kids you might want to practice outdoors or in the garage. Swing paddles, flying balls and kids don't mix very well indoors, and if they see parents doing it, they probably think that they have a legal license to follow suite.

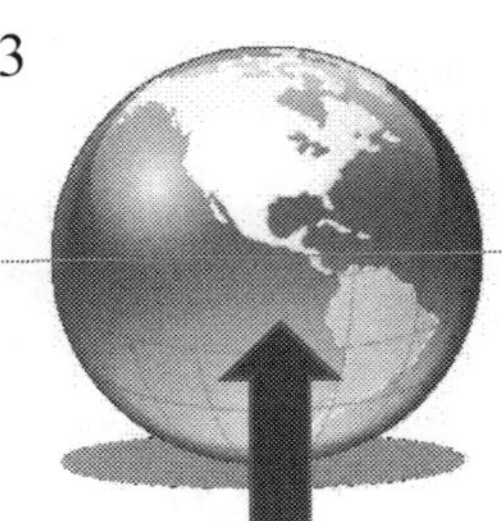

Contact ball below the equator!

Cues & Errors: Dinking in Doubles

Teaching Cues:	Common Errors:
1. Position the body square to the ball with knees at a relaxed bend and the paddle out in front 2. Move your feet to position body 3. With little backswing contact the ball below the equator in the southern hemisphere. 4. Swing toward line of target with firm wrist 5. Don't choke the paddle 6. Watch the ball hit the paddle 7. Use your ambient vision to determine position of your opponents 8. Lift the ball over the net about 6-12 inches with an emphasis on knee extension 9. After the stroke, change your focus to your opponents paddle 10. Return to proper court position to maximize coverage with paddle near chest high in case of a smash return	1. Sleepy feet and reaching for the ball 2. Hitting the ball too close to the body 3. No knee bend 4. Arms and hand too tense 5. Using too much wrist 6. Contacting ball at the equator 7. Not preparing for the return 8. Loss of patience

Skill Strategy: Partners in Sync

As in the drop shot, partners should keep moving together so they don't leave any wide gaps between them. Most of the points lost in the dink game are caused by unforced errors. If the ball bounces up at the level of or below the net, the preferred shot is a dink! A Velcro tie would work well here also.

Snap Shot: Dink Shot

Dink Drills: If you want to get better, you have to drill!

1. Dink 2 Ball Drill-Start off easy…but not too easy!
2. Dink Short Angle-You'll see this shot a lot in doubles.
3. The Dink Shuffle-You got to learn how to move those feet!
4. Dink 1 vs 2 Drill-Great drill for when you're waiting for the 4th to arrive.
5. Dink 2 Ball Chair Drill-End of the day and little tired? This is the drill for you.
6. Dink 4 Chair Drill-If No. 5 is too easy, try this one.

Dink Drill Videos:

Video 4.1: Dink 2 Ball Drill – 1.0 speed

Video 4.2: Dink Short Angle – 1.0 speed

Video 4.3: The Dink Shuffle - .50 speed

Video 4.4: Dink 1 vs 2 Drill – 1.0 speed

Video 4.5: Dink 2 Ball Chair Drill – 1.0 speed

Video 4.6: Dink 4 Chair Drill – 1.0 speed

Student Assignment No. 4.1: With a partner count how many consecutive dink shots you can hit. The instructor may set a specific time in which to complete the task. Only count the number of dink returns that you successfully make. Ideally, you should work in groups of 3 with the third person observing and filling out the performance score sheet after completion of the drill.

DINK SHOT - PERFORMANCE SCORE SHEET

Name:________________________ Scorer's Name:____________________ Date:__________

Skill Segment:	**Score: 0,1,2**
1. Happy feet	
2. Eyes on the ball to contact	
3. Firm wrist at contact	
4. Leg extension at contact	
6. Contact away from body	
7. Clearance of ball 6-12 inches	
8. Return to proper court position	
9. Paddle returned to chest high	
10. Smiling and having fun	
Skill Score (20 max. pts)	
Number of consecutive dink shots (xx pts)	
Total Score (xx pts)	
Scoring: 0 = Needs more practice 1= Good but needs a little more consistency 2 = Mastered	

ADVANCED KITCHEN SHOTS FOR DOUBLES

1. **The Cobra**: An aggressive hit off the dink to the opponent's body.
   a. If your opponent drops his/her paddle below the net height in anticipation of a dink return, it just might be time for a Cobra strike if the ball is at least net high.
   b. Go through the initial motions of hitting a dink shot, but instead, do a fast flick of the ball into your opponent's body about 9 inches above the navel or toward the paddle side of the body. A backhand block is slightly easier than a forehand block in this position. If you keep the ball at upper belly height and miss, the ball still might stay in play.
   c. Be ready for a quick return with your paddle positioned chest high.
   d. Be patient and look for an opening.

Cobra Dink to Volley Drill Video:

Video 4.7: Dink to Volley Cobra Drill – 1.0 speed

2. **The Hallway or The Avenue**: A firm shot that goes between you opponents.
   a. While dinking, work your opponent to one side of the court. If his partner does not move to the cover the center opening, use the same stroke as a dink, but push the ball a little harder right down the "The Hallway" or "The Avenue."
   b. Don't hit the ball too hard, as it will probably fly long out of play.

Park Avenue in Arches National Park. Look for the gap between opponents.

3. Lob off the dink:

a. If your opponent has a difficult time moving back or converting on overheads, a lob off the dink might just do the trick.
b. If not used too often, this shot will catch players off guard.
c. Using the same stroke as the dink, push the ball up and over your opponent's backhand side.
d. This should not be a very high shot, but just high enough to clear the outstretched arm and paddle. Done correctly this shot will not give your opponent time to camp under the ball and may result in a weak overhead return.

Dink to Lob Drill Video:

Video 4.8: Dink, Dink, Lob Drill – 1.0 speed

SKILL NO. 5 VOLLEYS

Overview: **Be unto thine opponent as a wall of fire**. A volley is hitting the ball out of the air before it bounces and is another essential pickleball skill. There are multiple variations of the volley: 1. it can be hit soft, short and with spin, 2. it can be hit firmly flat and deep or, 3. it can be blocked back into the kitchen. A volley may be initiated off an opponent's ground stroke, overhead smash, volley, or a deep dink shot.

5.1 BASIC VOLLEY

5.1 Cues & Errors: Basic Volley (waist to shoulder height)

Teaching Cues:	Common Errors:
1. Position the body square to the ball before it is struck by your opponent 2. Athletic position with a relaxed bend in the knees 3. Paddle should be shoulder high in front of body (It is quicker to move the paddle down than to bring it up.) 4. A neutral handshake grip with the "V" made by thumb and index finger on top of grip is preferred 5. For most cases the paddle should be positioned on edge in line with the body's midline (This will facilitate both forehand and backhand volleys. Occasionally, if you are pulled off to the side of the court near the kitchen, and your dominant hand is toward center court, you might turn the paddle to a forehand volley ready position.) 6. Don't choke the paddle 7. Firm wrist 8. Keep wrist below tip of paddle (You're not scooping ice cream!) 9. Little to no backswing 10. Watch the ball hit the paddle (Use your ambient vision to determine position of your opponents.) 11. Hit through the ball 12. If there is time, such as a volley coming off a ground stroke, slightly turn the shoulders toward the paddle and shift weight to the front foot (Jab step) (It is almost always a good idea to be aggressive by moving your weight into the volley.)	1. Eyes off the ball 2. Too much of a backswing (In your ambient vision you should always see your paddle.) 3. Dropping tip of paddle below the wrist

Skill Strategy: Paddle Position

It is essential that the tip of the paddle is always above the wrist and in a ready position at chest height. The wrist should be firm and in a laid back position for the forehand volley. Lowering the tip of the paddle below the wrist will usually result in a big Lollypop return to your opponent...Lollypops are not good for your health.

Snap Shot: Basic Volley Position

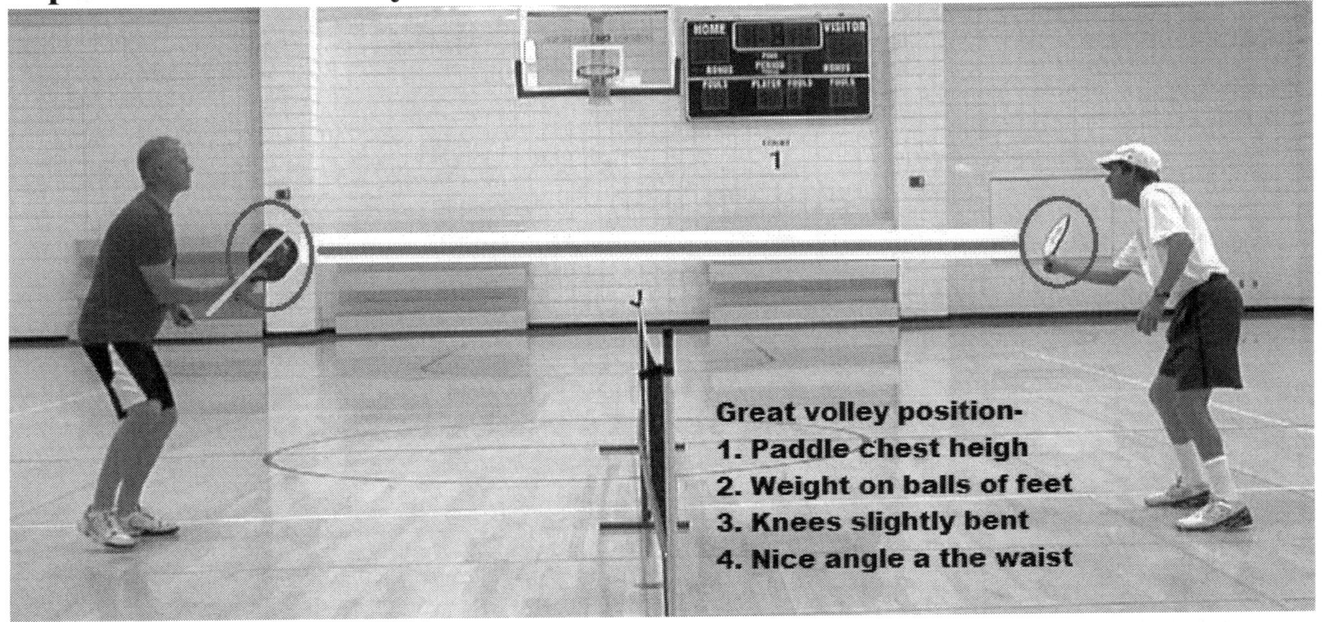

5.1 Basic Volley Drills:

1. Volley 1 on 1 at the Net
2. Volley Slide Drill
2. Volley 1 on 1 Multiple Balls
3. Volley 1 vs 2: You can start with one ball and progress to two or more. Multiple ball drills are a great way to develop the effective use of your ambient vision system.

5.1 Basic Volley Videos:

Video 5.1: Volley 1 on 1 with Shuffle – 1.0 speed

Video 5.2: Volley Slide Drill – 1.0 speed

Video 5.3: Volley 1 on 1 Multiple Balls – 1.0 speed

Video 5.4: Volley 1 vs 2 Drill – 1.0 speed

5.2 SOFT BACKSPIN OR DROP VOLLEY (Advanced Technique)

When your opponent is deep to the baseline and you are volleying a ground stroke, a good occasional strategy is to hit a soft backspin volley near the kitchen (A drop volley with backspin). (You will probably find more opportunities to use this shot in singles than doubles play.)

5.2 Cues & Errors: Soft Backspin/Drop Volley

Teaching Cues:	Common Errors:
1. Paddle starts well above the wrist 2. Backswing is very short 3. Swing down and forward brushing the back/underneath side of the ball 4. Open the paddle face enough to give the ball an upward/forward flight 5. Follow-through should be an upward arch (The path of the paddle should look like an upside down rainbow.) 	1. Paddle face is too open = pop-up 2. Contact point is too high on the ball = net ball 3. Too much of a backswing

Snap Shot: Drop Volley

5.2 Drop Volley Videos:

Video 5.5: Drop Volley (1) - .50 speed
Video 5.6: Drop Volley (2) - .50 speed

5.3 APPROACH SHOT TO VOLLEY

An approach shot is usually a deep shot that causes your opponent to chase or stretch for the ball, and is the key to positioning yourself for a point winning volley.

5.3 Cues & Errors: Approach Shot to Volley

Teaching Cues:	Common Errors:
1. Move your feet to position body for an easy ground stroke 2. Return the ball deep to your opponent's weak side 3. Follow the ball path by quickly moving your body to the short service line 4. Execute a split-stop (both feet landing together with the body in perfect balance) 5. The paddle should be chest high and in front of the body with a firm wrist and eye on the ball	1. Paddle in too low of a position 2. Running through the ball without a split-stop

Snap Shot: Split-Stop

5.3 Approach Shot to Volley Video:

Video 5.7: Approach Volley - .50 speed

5.4 LOW VOLLEY

The low volley is another stroke that needs to be mastered if one is to move up to a higher level of play. This stroke may present itself while coming to the net following an approach shot, or at the no volley line when attempting to pick off a long dink.

5.4 Cues & Errors: Low Volley

Teaching Cues:	Common Errors:
1. Move your feet to position body in a balanced position. 2. Bend your knees to keep your tail low 3. Wrist should be in a laid-back position 4. Paddle should be in a near horizontal position 5. Depending on the court position of your opponent(s), effective returns may be short angles, short dinks or deeper to open areas 6. For short returns, soften your grip and let the paddle absorb the impact of the ball	1. Paddle below the hand and wrist, which often leads to a pop-up 2. Legs too straight, tail too high

Snap Shot: Low Volley

Low Volley Video:

Video 5.8: Low Volley - .50 speed

5.5 BACKHAND SWEEP

Occasionally, you might be a target victim and experience a hard volley to the body. No problem. The backhand sweep just might save you, because it is one of the quickest defensive movements known to the pickleball world.

5.5 Cues & Errors: Backhand Sweep

Teaching Cues:	Common Errors:
1. Ready position with paddle on edge in front of the body chest high 2. Paddle above the wrist 3. Handshake grip 4. Simple lift your elbow high and flatten out the paddle for an amazingly fast backhand return	1. Paddle to the side of the body and below chest level

Snap Shot: Backhand Sweep (Protector)

Backhand Sweep Videos:

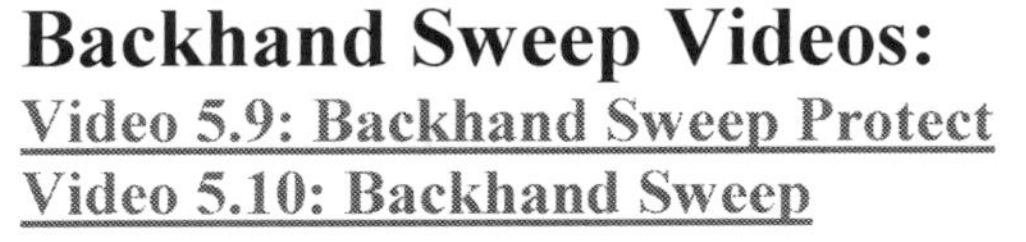
Video 5.9: Backhand Sweep Protect
Video 5.10: Backhand Sweep

Student Assignment No. 5.1: With a partner count how many consecutive short volleys you can hit. Only count the number of volleys that you return.

Student Assignment No. 5.2: Have your partner hit you 10 balls from the baseline. You will volley each ball to a designated target. Ideally, you should work in groups of 3 with the third person observing and filling out the performance score sheet.

VOLLEY - PERFORMANCE SCORE SHEET

Name:____________________ Scorer's Name:__________________ Date:________

Skill Segment:	Score: 0,1,2
1. Happy feet	
2. Eyes on the ball to contact	
3. Firm wrist at contact	
4. Tip of paddle even or above wrist height	
5. Paddle and hand chest high	
6. Very little back swing	
7. Return to proper court position	
8. Control and consistency of volley	
9. Attempted drop volley with some success	
10. Smiling & having fun	
Skill Score (20 max. pts)	
Number of consecutive dink shots (xx pts)	
Total Score (xx pts)	
Scoring: 0 = Needs more practice 1= Good but needs a little more consistency 2 = Mastered	

SKILL NO. 6 HALF-VOLLEY

Overview: The half-volley is primarily a defensive shot where the ball bounces at your feet. This most commonly happens when a player is coming to the kitchen area from the baseline and the returning ball is hit low to the feet in the mid-court area. Footwork and body position are crucial elements in this stroke. Most half-volleys should be hit with the goal of dropping or dinking the ball into the kitchen. If you are slow moving or indecisive this may happen quite often in singles play and occasionally in doubles.

Cues & Errors - Half-Volley

Teaching Cues:	Common Errors:
1. Use a "split stop" (See Skill Strategy below) as opponent is about to hit a return (This allows you to change direction and react to the return.) 2. Step toward direction of ball (For right handers: left leg on forehand shots and right leg on back-hand shots. For you lefty's, just the opposite.) 3. Backswing is very short 4. Drop your tail by bending the knees 5. Drop the side of paddle behind where the ball will hit the court (Tip of the paddle should be more horizontal than vertical. You'll probably have to do considerable bending with knees and waist to get into this position.) 6. Follow-through should be short with paddle turned slightly upward	1. Not setting feet (running through the ball) 2. Bending at waist, without knee bend 3. Tip of paddle drops below wrist 4. Swing amplitude is too great

Skill Strategy: Split Stop

Split Stop is the easiest way to get set for a return when on the move. This step is accomplished by landing on the balls of your feet at the same time and in parallel position. It is initiated at the moment when your opponent begins to swing at the ball. When landing, the knees should be slightly bent, back straight, head up and hands in front. Now you can move in either direction quickly and decisively.

Snap Shot: Half-Volley (Approach)

Approach: Have paddle out in front, with wrist in an extended position.

Pre-contact: 1. Bend the knees and get your tail low, 2. Stop your momentum with a split-stop before contact.

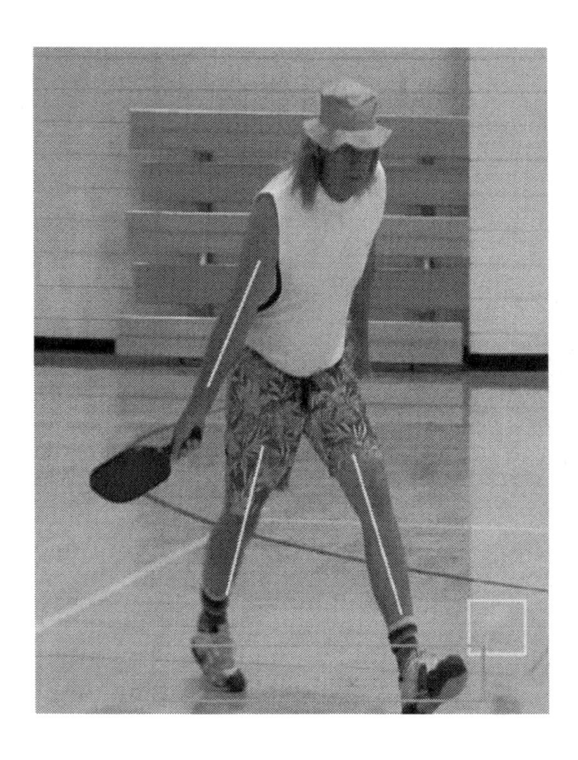

Snap Shot: Half-Volley (Contact/Follow-Through)

Contact: 1. Plant your feet if you have time…don't run through the ball, 2. Focus on the ball, 3. Bend your knees, 4. Wrist in an extended position, **5. Contact the ball out in front of the feet.**

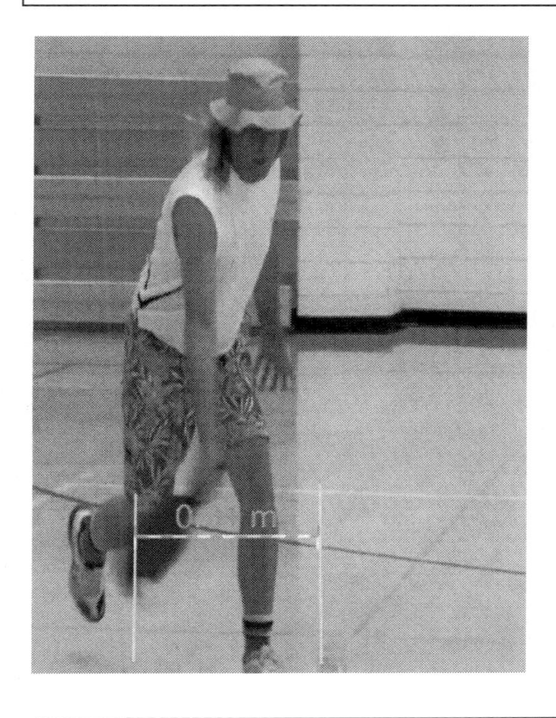

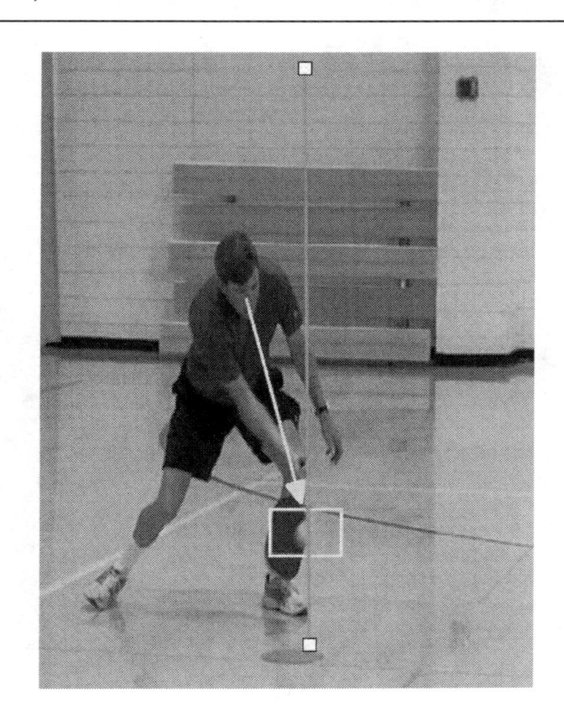

Follow-through: 1. Keep momentum moving toward target, 2. Keep wrist in an extended position.

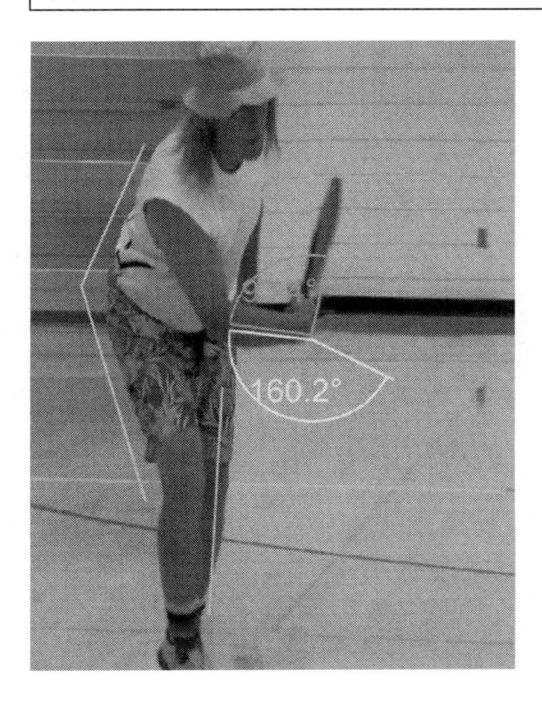

Snap Shot: Half-Volley (Backhand)

Half-Volley Video:

Video 6.1: Half Volley Bubba vs Tim - .25 speed

Video 6.2: Half Volley Backhand - .50 speed

Half-Volley Drill:

1. Throw at feet Drill

Half-Volley Drill Video:

Video 6.3: Half Volley Drill

Student Assignment 6.1: Standing 3 steps in from the baseline have your partner feed you 10 balls at your feet. Count how many half-volleys you can hit in play. Count one point if ball lands in play and 2 points in it lands in a target area. Have your other partner fill out the Half-Volley Performance Score Sheet.

HALF-VOLLEY - PERFORMANCE SCORE SHEET

Name:________________________ Scorer's Name:____________________

Date:__________

Skill Segment:	**Score: 0,1,2**
1. Happy feet	
2. Eyes on the ball at contact	
3. Little if no backswing	
4. Firm wrist at contact	
5. Tip of paddle more horizontal than vertical	
Skill Score x 2 (20 max. pts)	
Number half-volleys in target area 2 pts each (20 max pts)	
Number of half-volleys in play but not in target area 1 pt. each (10 max pts)	
Total Score (40 max. pts)	
Scoring: 0 = Needs more practice 1= Good but needs a little more consistency 2 = Mastered	

SKILL NO. 7 OVERHEAD SMASH

Overview: The overhead smash is one of the most spectacular and fun shots in pickleball. It's like eating dessert before the main meal. The mechanics are very similar to hitting an overhead serve in tennis or throw an overhand baseball.

Cues & Errors - Overhead Smash

Teaching Cues:	Common Errors:
1. First movement from the ready position is a drop-step backwards from the dominant side 2. Turn hips and shoulders perpendicular to the net (If the drop step is done correctly the hip and shoulder turn will follow quite naturally and will be pointing to the target.) 3. Raise the paddle elbow to shoulder height 4. Use adjustment steps to position body behind the ball (When the lob is deep, use crossover steps to get into position. If you try to backpedal there is a good chance you'll end up on your butt.) 5. Try to position the body so that the ball is coming down over the front shoulder 6. Chin up, front arm pointing to the ball (If you pull your chin down during the swing, you can bet the ball is heading to the net.) 7. Contact by releasing the wrist with slight pronation (Pronation is when the wrist and forearm are rotated toward little finger…This is like throwing a Karate punch. The pickleball overhead is more like the badminton smash rather than the tennis overhead in that the wrist is released from a firm position.) 8. **Elbow must remain behind the ball at contact**! If not, the ball will probably hit the back fence or fly out of the stadium	1. No drop-step 2. No body turn 3. Back peddling 4. Elbow in front of ball at contact

9. Follow-through: The arm will remain shoulder high with the wrist and tip of paddle pointing down	

Snap Shot: Overhead Smash (1)

Snap Shot: Overhead Smash (2)

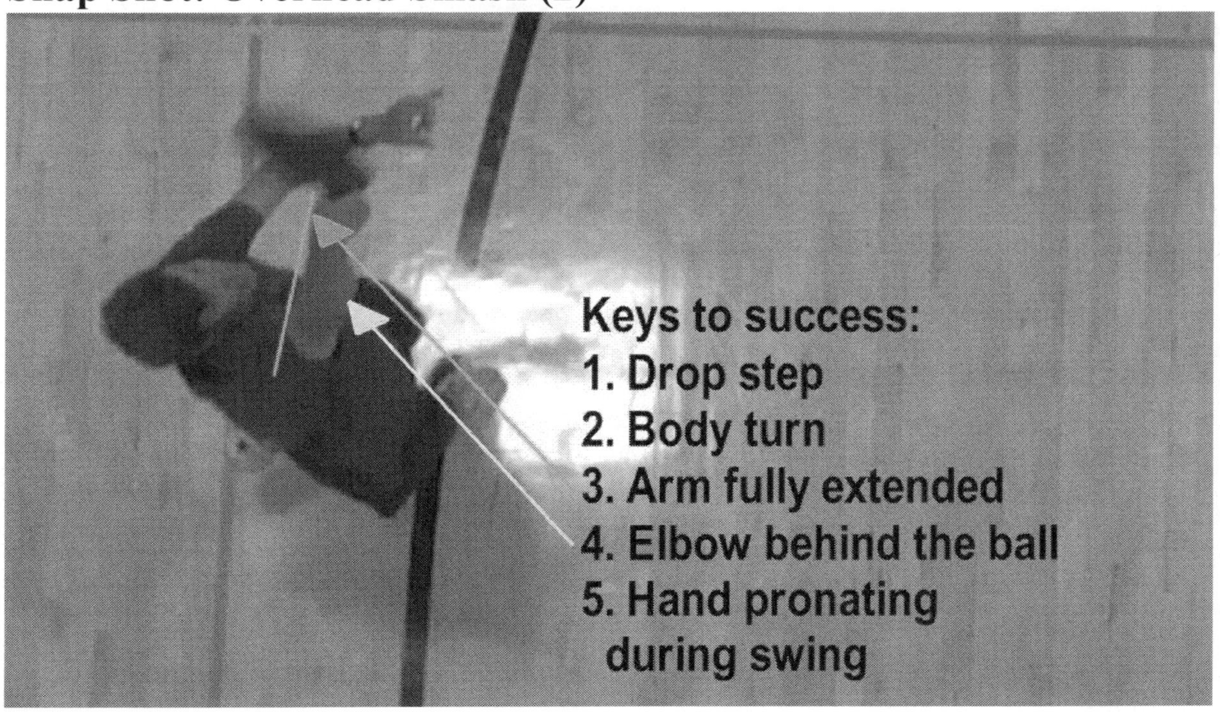

Snap Shot: Overhead Stromotion

Skill Strategy: Returning a Lob

Always try to hit a smash rather than letting it bounce. If you let it bounce you give your opponents time to get to the net and you now have to hit a very long ground stroke or a difficult deep lob. Not a good situation.

Skill Strategy: Return of Smash

If you see an overhead coming, get to the baseline as fast as you can. Playing doubles you both need to move as a pair. If you can get to the smash, your 2 best stroke options are a lob or a drop shot into the kitchen.

Smash Videos:

Video 7.1: Overhead Back View - .50 speed

Video 7.2: Overhead Birdseye - .50 speed

Video 7.3: Overhead Upper body - .25 speed
Video 7.4: Overhead Cross-Over - .50 speed
Video 7.5: Overhead Shuffle - .50 speed
Video 7.6: Overhead Cross-Over vs Shuffle - .25 speed

Smash Drill:

1. Smash drill with multiple feeds

Smash Drill Videos:

Video 7.7: Overhead Smash Drill – Multiple Feeds - 1.0 speed

Video 7.8: Overhead Drill - 1.0 speed

Student Assignment 7.1: Standing at the no volley zone, have your partner feed you 10 balls with an underhand toss high and over your head. The feeder should stand off the court near the net post on the paddle side of the hitter. Count how many smashes you can hit in play. Have your other partner fill out the Smash Performance Score Sheet.

OVERHEAD SMASH - PERFORMANCE SCORE SHEET

Name:________________________ Scorer's Name:____________________

Date:__________

Skill Segment:	**Score: 0,1,2**
1. Drop-Step	
2. Should rotation	
3. Elbow up (shoulder height)	
4. Plant back foot	
5. Chin up	
6. Elbow behind ball at contact	
7. Follow-Through: Arm at shoulder height	
Skill Score x 2 (28 max. pts)	
Number overheads that land in play x 2 (20 max. pts)	
Total Score (48 max. pts)	
Scoring: 0 = Needs more practice 1= Good but needs a little more consistency 2 = Mastered	

SKILL NO. 8 LOB

Overview: The lob is probably one of the least used and practiced shots in pickleball but it can be a very effective shot to get you out of a difficult situation, push your opponent(s) out of position, change the pace of the game, or just to give yourself more time to recover. There are two classes of lobs: defensive and offensive. The main difference between the two is the height and from where on the court the lob is initiated.

Delicate Arch-Arches National Park. The lob should be a delicate arc over your opponent's head.

Skill Strategy: Lob

A defensive lob is used when you are pulled out of position deep toward the baseline or wide from the sideline. Contact the ball beneath the equator and push it high and deep to your opponents back court. If possible the shot should be placed over the non-dominant shoulder. When performed correctly this shot will give you ample time to return to an optimal position on the court.

There are two ideal positions after hitting the lob:

1. If the ball is short, you're in trouble…retreat to the baseline and "hunker-down" (take your partner with you if you're playing doubles). You "hunker-down" by facing the ball in an athletic position (linebacker stance) with the paddle out in front at waist height ready for a hard smash. As you are retreating you might say a prayer or two.
2. If your lob is deep, advance with your partner to the kitchen line, snarl and wait for the next shot.

An offensive lob should be a shot that surprises your opponent. It is not as high as the defensive lob and can be hit with some top spin over the backhand side. This shot is usually attempted after an exchange of dinks at the net.

Return of lob: In doubles, both players should go back to retrieve a lob which is normally returned by the forehand player with another lob if it is allowed to bounce. If the lob is short, communicate who will attempt an overhead smash. Good communication is essential in doubles play. This is a social game; talk with each other.

Cues & Errors - Lob

Teaching Cues:	Common Errors:
1. Position your body so that you can step forward into the shot (This requires happy feet.) 2. Step toward ball with knees slightly flexed (You're probably tired of hearing about feet and knees but get used to it…there are too many people that like sleepy feet and locked knees, and they need to be reminded.) 3. Backswing is very short or non-existent 4. Let the paddle head drop well below the ball 5. Stroke with a firm wrist using your arm, shoulder and legs to push the ball up and over your opponents 6. For top-spin brush quickly up the backside of the ball 7. Follow-through should be upward and in direction of the target	1. Not using feet to position body 2. Bending at waist, without knee bend 3. Too much wrist involvement

Snap Shot: Lob

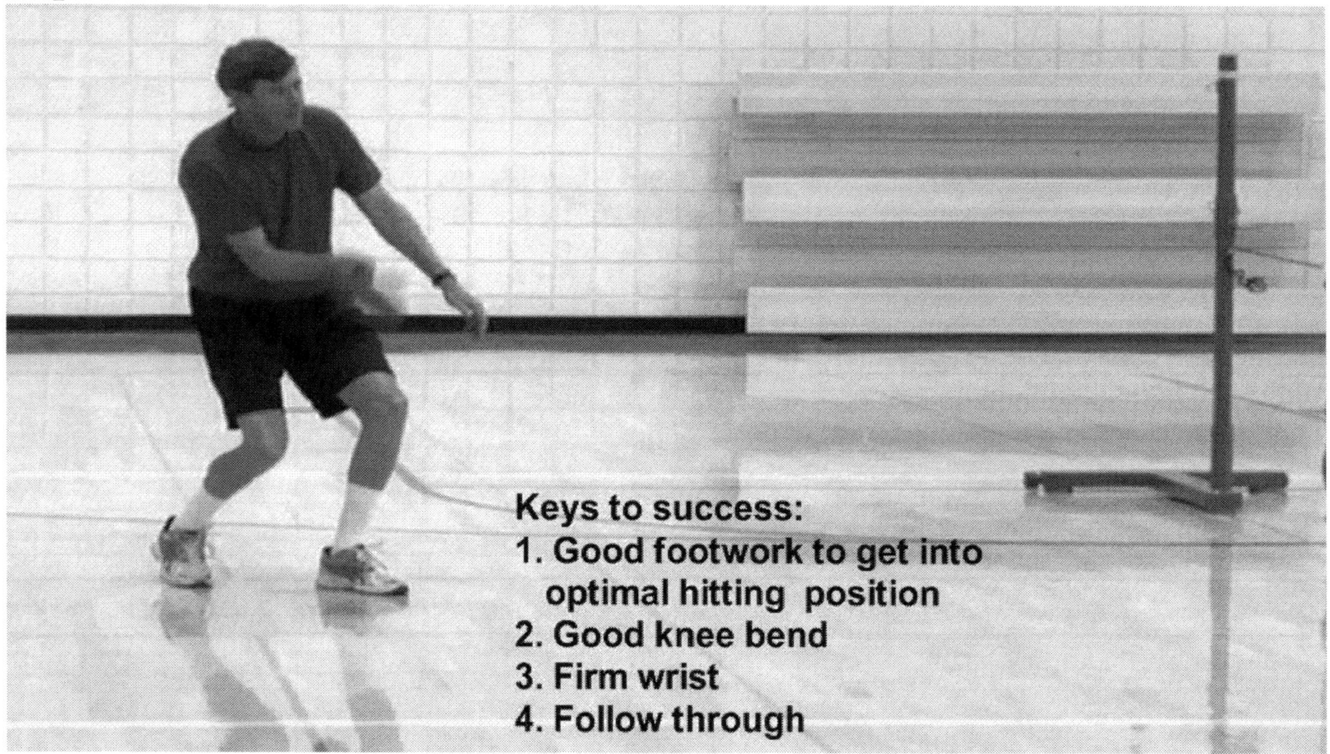

Lob Videos:

Video 8.1: Basic Lob Technique - .50 speed

Video 8.2: Lob off Dink - .50 speed

Lob Drill:

1. Lob Drill with Partner: You can use multiple balls at the same time to make this drill more challenging.

Lob Drill Video:

Video 8.3: Long Lob Drill – 1.0 speed

Student Assignment 8.1: Standing at the no volley line, have your partner feed you 10 dink balls in the kitchen. Return 5 lobs to the left hand corner target and 5 to the right hand target. 2. Standing at the baseline, have your partner feed you 10 high tosses that bounce near the baseline. Return 5 lobs to the left hand target and 5 to the right hand target. Have your other partner fill out the Lob Performance Score Sheet.

LOB - PERFORMANCE SCORE SHEET

Name:________________________ Scorer's Name:____________________

Date:__________

Skill Segment:	**Score: 0,1,2**
1. Moving feet to position body	
2. Knee bend	
3. Firm wrist at contact	
4. Some top spin	
5. Follow-through upward and toward target	
Skill Score x2 (20 max. pts)	
Number lobs that land in play (20 max. pts)	
Total Score (40 max. pts)	
Scoring: 0 = Needs more practice 1= Good but needs a little more consistency 2 = Mastered	

BOOK III: MORE DRILLS, GAMES AND ACTIVITIES

PRACTICE & COMBINATION DRILLS

Overview: Most good combination drills will script or require a certain number of required hits before a point is played out. It makes no sense to practice a shot or sequence of shots if they have no relevance or application to a "real" game. However, if you just want to have fun anything goes…after all isn't that how pickleball was conceived?

1. Serve, Return, Drop Drill (Doubles)

a. Team A serves to Team B. Team B returns the serve to a specific deep target and both B-Team members advance to the no-volley line.
b. As Team A initiates a shot, both members of B-Team execute a perfect "split stop" and prepare for a return.
c. After A-Team members hit the 3rd shot, they move together depending on how well their attempted drop shot is executed (If the drop shot is headed toward the kitchen…good, both come to the net; if the shot is long and you're going to get killed…both stay back…it won't hurt as bad).
d. Play out the point and then Team B will serve and repeat the drill.

2. Lob, Smash, Return (Singles or Doubles)

a. Player A starts at a mid-court position. Player B will start at the kitchen line.
b. Player A will initiate the drill by lobbing to Player B, who will position himself/herself with correct form under the ball and return a medium hard smash to the feet of Player A (Don't try to hurt your partner yet…you'll have other opportunities later).
c. Player A after hunkering down will attempt to return the smash into the kitchen.
d. Play out the point.

LEAD-UP GAMES

1. Half-Court Singles

a. This is a great game for practicing control and consistency for the serve, return and drop shot. It is also very good for developing patience at the net. If you only have 2 people and wish to practice your double-skills, you can't beat this game.
b. The playing area is one-half of the court divided lengthwise and following the mid-service line to the baseline.
c. The three required shots are 1. Deep serve, 2. Deep Return with advancement to the kitchen, 3. Drop shot, then play out the point.

Lead-up Game Video:

Video III.1: Half-Court Singles – 1.0 speed

2. The Kitchen Game

a. A simple but very effective game that will teach placement and control of the dink shot.
b. Four players (2 on each side of the net) will hit diagonal dink shots to opponents on the opposite side within the ½ kitchen area.
c. There will be 2 balls played at the same time.
d. If the ball lands outside of the kitchen (all lines are in) a point is awarded to the receiving player. Play will continue by initiating another dink.
e. If the 2 balls collide, no points are scored and play continues.
f. Each player will keep their own individual score.
g. When time is called, both teams will add up their scores. The losing team will wash dishes or make cookies for the winners.

3. Modified Games

Modified games will increase focus and concentration on every point and help create a more competitive, game-like environment (TARGET CONTEXT). If you are preparing for match play you might also include rewards and consequences such as buying lunch, cleaning the bathroom, washing the car, doing the laundry etc.

h. Play games to 5 points instead of 11.
i. Triple the first point in an eleven point game.
j. Play games to 2 points win by 2. Keep track of number of games won. This would work well for King's/Queen's court rotation.
k. Play regular games to 11 points but subtract a point for every unforced error or any ball in the net.

BOOK IV: GAME STRATEGIES

Skill Strategy: Keep the ball in Play

A great many points in pickleball are won on unforced errors. Make your opponent work for every point (Who knows, he/she may give you a gift). There are 3 strategies that will help you cut down on unforced errors: 1. Don't try to hit a better shot than is necessary, 2. When hitting a difficult shot, think of the net being 6" higher (Many unforced errors are in the net.), 3. If your opponent is on the baseline, a crosscourt return has more area to land in and center of the net will be an inch lower. Remember, if you return one more ball than your opponent…you win the point.

Skill Strategy: If it works…

If a strategy or shot is working well for you, don't change it. If it's not working, try something different. The same actions will usually produce similar results. Have alternate strategies and don't be afraid to use them if things are not going well. A time out is a good time to rethink strategies and regroup. It may also cool off your opponent.

SINGLES

Overview: The singles game is not a doubles game played with two less people on a same size court. What stroke to hit, how to hit it, where to hit it, and where to move are critical decisions that are constantly being challenged in singles. It is a much more physically demanding game that requires a much higher level of agility, quickness, and endurance fitness than doubles. Besides that, there is no one else to blame for a poor showing, which in itself creates a lot more stress.

1. SERVE

a. First match serve-To start a game, use your most consistent serve. As the game progresses and you calm your butterflies and gain more confidence, you can hit harder serves with more spin and precise placement.
b. Center position-Serve from a position near center baseline. This will place you in a good home position ready for the return.
c. Keep returner back-Hitting deep serves will keep returner back.
d. Create a weak return-Hitting a variety of deep serves with alternating spins and angles will help to create a weak return.

2. RETURN OF SERVE & GROUND STROKES

a. Position-Assume a position just behind the baseline that bisects the angle to which the serve may be hit. If you are quick enough and the server doesn't have a hard controlled serve you may position yourself closer to the backhand side and plan to hit a more aggressive forehand return.
b. Primary and secondary targets on return of serve or ground strokes-Before the serve you should have your primary and secondary targets already picked out. The primary target will usually be the one you can hit confidently with a forehand stroke. The secondary target will be the one you will go for if the serve forces you to hit backhand or pulls you

into a stretched position. This shot might be a medium paced shot deep to the center of the court (A center court return decreases the angle that your opponent can use).

c. Adjust-As the game progresses you can make adjustments based on the type, force and spin of your opponent's serves and ground strokes that he/she is most consistently using.
d. Targets-For ground strokes, targets are similar to return of serve targets and include: short angle to side of court, deep backhand corner, deep medium pace to center to allow you to get to kitchen etc.
e. Strengths vs weaknesses-You need to decide what your opponent's weaknesses and strengths are and how you can match that with your strengths. If you don't match up well, try to force your opponent to use his/her weakest shot.
f. Move diagonally-If the serve or return is wide, quickly move on a forward diagonal line to cut it off and reduce the distance and angle you have to cover.
g. Deep returns-To slow down or prevent your opponent from reaching a more offensive position at the kitchen and reduce the hitting angle which decreases the area that you have to cover, hit your returns deep. Depth is more effective than power.

3. COURT POSITIONS

a. Home base-Establishing a "home base" is essential when waiting for your opponent's return shot. For deep ground strokes, if the ball is being hit from the center of the court then your home base should be center court just behind the baseline.
b. Bisect the angle-When hitting baseline to baseline, if the ball is being returned from the left corner you should position yourself a foot or so to the right of center court. If returning from the right corner move slightly to the left to bisect the possible angle of return.
c. Stay out of midcourt-Midcourt is commonly referred to as "no man's land," and should be avoided like the "kitchen," unless you are really good at low or half-volleys.

4. NET PLAY

a. Approach shot-In singles, the first key is to decide when to come to the net. A good deep approach shot to your opponent's backhand side presents a good opportunity to follow the shot to the net. Any shot (including short angles) that stretches your opponent out can also work as a good approach shot.
b. Cover sideline first-One of the first considerations in advancing to the net in singles is to cover as much return territory as possible. This is done by establishing a home base near the no-volley line, a little off-center toward the side from which the ball will be returned. Make sure you cover the near sideline first.
c. A split stop just as your opponent begins his/her swing is crucial when coming to the net. This will get you into position to move in any direction.
d. Paddle focus-Your eyes should be focusing on your opponent's paddle position which will help you anticipate the directional flight of the return.
e. Move quickly-You should be moving toward the ball as soon as or before the ball is struck. Don't wait for the ball to cross the net.
f. Move diagonally forward to decrease the angle of return and shorten the distance you need to cover.
g. Deeper and flatter for high volleys-Most errors from midcourt volleys that are at waist height or higher are put in the net. To avoid this, hit flatter and deeper volleys.
h. Drop volleys can be very effective if your opponent is deep and moving toward the side court and hits a return that is forcing you to contact the ball below the net. Remember to open the paddle face and use very little follow-through.
i. Return the lob with an overhead, but try not to hit it too hard. Focus on placement rather than speed.

5. GENERAL CONSIDERATIONS

a. Focus on present challenge-Concentration is impaired when a player is faced with a stressful or pressured event or is thinking about a bad shot or bad call. Focusing on the next two-shot combination (i.e. serve + shot angle to backhand or deep return to backhand + drop volley) will help to redirect concentration.
b. Play within your capabilities-Play your most consistent shot most of the time. Good player will rarely try a difficult shot if an easy one will accomplish the same thing. Over-hitting is a common mistake that usually occurs at the beginning of a match or when playing superman.
c. Make your opponent hit a winner-As pressure builds during a match, unforced errors become more common. Make your opponent hit the ball to beat you.
d. Aggressive opportunities-When playing a very good opponent look for those rare opportunities to play an aggressive shot and go for it…don't be an Elmer Milktoast and back off.
e. The short ball-Be ready for the short ball and take a couple of steps in the court if you force your opponent to stretch for a shot. Take the shot early on the up-bounce rather than waiting for the top or back half of the bounce. This will give your opponent less time to react and get back to home base.
f. Set-up the killer-The set-up shot before the winning shot is a thing of beauty and should be given as much credit as the winner. Good chess players and pickleball players should be planning several strokes in advance. Have patience, a good set-up shot will make the winning shot a lot easier.
g. First points-The first points in a game are always important as it puts added pressure on your opponent and more pressure usually translates into more unforced errors.
h. Final points- The final points in a match are often the hardest to win because you now have a lion backed into a corner and he/she will come out fighting like mad. AND/OR you have lost concentration and are beginning to think about your next game, lunch or calling your stock broker.
i. Regroup-If you have lost focus or are becoming frustrated with the game you need to regroup. Taking extra time or calling a time out will often help you get back on track. If you are getting killed, play with a purpose in mind (i.e. hit good shots, with good placement and better consistency, practice a different game-plan, etc.). If you lose, you lose, the sun will come up in the morning and you can re-read this book with purpose in mind.
j. Avoid negative body language-Negative body language (slumping shoulders, head down, and knuckles dragging on the ground) feeds your opponent with extra resolve to finish you off and put you out of your misery. It also indicates that you are focused on the past and are not ready to concentrate on the next point. Take a deep breath, square up your shoulders and be a man or woman. Don't be a wimp.

DOUBLES

Overview: **Be unto thine opponent as an impregnable wall.** The doubles game is not a singles game played with two more people, but it does incorporate many of the skills and strategies of single competition. Positioning is the name of game for doubles. There are also a few benefits that set it apart from singles: 1. It is more sociable and can lead to lasting friendships, 2. It is physically less demanding, and 3. You have a built-in scapegoat.

Some of the double's strategies are the same as single's strategies but are reprinted for the benefit of those who have skipped the single's strategy section of the book. For the rest of you, repetition is a fundamental principle of motor learning.

The Great Wall-Arches National Park. Remember, victory follows close on heals of those who are first to the net in doubles.

1. SERVING TEAM

a. Both Back-The serving team will start with both players at the baseline. Because of the double-bounce rule the serving team must let the return of serve bounce before hitting the 3rd shot.
b. First match serve-Have the most effective and consistent server start the game with their most consistent serve. As the game progresses and you calm your butterflies, and gain more confidence, both of you can hit harder serves with more spin and precise placement.
c. Position-The server in doubles has more options from where to start the serve than a singles player. He/she may start closer to the sideline or the center-court position depending on desirable angles that better expose the weaknesses of the returning opponent. For example, if serving from the add side (left-side) to a right-handed opponent who has a weak backhand, the server may start closer to the sideline in order to access a better angle to the returner's backhand.
d. Keep returner back by hitting deep serves. This will give you a better opportunity to hit the critical 3rd shot at the returner's feet when he/she is on the move.
e. Create a weak return by hitting a variety of deep serves with alternating spins and angles. A short return creates all kinds of opportunities for the serving team to hit easier drop shots, passing shots, smashes and enables both partners to get to the net.
f. Both up on a weak return-If the return shot comes back short, both teammates should move forward in preparation for an approach shot to the person who is still back or is moving forward. If your partner refuses to come to the kitchen with you, change partners or change deodorant.

2. RETURNING TEAM

a. Start one up one back-The team receiving the serve should position the receiving player back slightly behind the baseline, with the partner in a forward position, a few steps back from the no-volley line.
b. Receiving position-Assume a position just behind the baseline that bisects the angle to which the serve may be hit. If you are quick enough and the server doesn't have a hard, controlled serve, you may position yourself closer to the backhand side and plan to hit a more aggressive forehand return.
c. Primary and secondary targets-Before the serve you should have your primary and secondary targets already picked out. The primary target will usually be the one you can hit confidently with a forehand stroke to the weakest player's backhand. The secondary target will be the one you will go for if the serve forces you to hit backhand or pulls you into a stretched position. This shot might be a medium paced shot deep to the center of the court. A center court return decreases the angle that your opponent can use and may create indecision for the opposing team. Most deep returns will delay your opponents from advancing to the net.
d. Adjust-As the game progresses you can make adjustments to your return based on the type, force and spin of the serves and ground strokes that your opponent is most consistently using.
e. Stay up or move back? The person in the forecourt has a very important decision to make on the return of serve. If he/she sees that the return is deep then he/she should remain at the kitchen and hope that the partner is focused enough to join the party. On the other hand if the return is weak and short, both partners should retreat toward the baseline and prepare for an aggressive approach shot. Don't retreat clear back to Kansas and get caught in a half-step. Remember to split-stop or get both feet under you so that you can cover short angles and drop shots.
f. Targets for ground strokes are similar to return of serve targets and include: short angle to side of court, deep backhand corner, and deep medium pace to center to allow you to get to kitchen.
g. Strengths vs weaknesses-You need to decide what your opponent's weaknesses and strengths are and how you can match them with your strengths. If you don't match up well, try to force your opponent to use his/her weakest shot.
h. Move diagonally-If the serve or return is wide, quickly move on a forward diagonal line to cut it off and reduce the distance and angle you have to cover.
i. A deep return will slow down or prevent your opposing team from reaching a better offensive position at the kitchen and reduce the hitting angle; which will decrease the area that you have to cover. Depth is more effective than power.

3. GENERAL COURT STRATEGIES

a. Cover the Hallway or Avenue-It is usually the forehand player's responsibility to cover the hallway (center-court). When there is a difference between skill levels of partners, they should communicate up front who has that responsibility.
b. Stay out of midcourt (halfway between baseline and kitchen), or commonly referred to as "no man's land" unless you are really good at low or half-volleys.
c. The 1/3 principle-When you pull your opponents wide to a sideline, you and your partner need to divide the court into thirds for proper coverage. The partner closest to the ball will cover down the line returns and 1/3 of the court. The other partner will cover the middle one-third. It will take a great shot or luck by your opponent to return to the unprotected area.

d. Who to hit to-Normally if you have a choice, you should hit to the less skilled opponent. However, whichever opponent makes a mistake is a good candidate for receiving the next shot. Many players will dwell on their current mistakes rather than the next point, which may adversely affect their performance.
e. Around the pole-It is legal and effective to step to the side of the kitchen and smash a wide and high dink shot. Make sure that the dink shot bounces higher than the height of the net and is wide enough to reach it by standing just to the side of the kitchen. Don't touch the net or pole with your body or paddle.
f. Poaching-is crossing onto your partner's side and intercepting the ball with a volley return near the kitchen. This is usually most effective when the poacher is moving to his/her forehand side, but can be performed successfully by more advanced players on either the forehand or backhand sides. Communication is critical for this move to be successful. Hand signals or verbal cues are effective communication strategies. Once you have committed to the move, you must complete the cross-over because your partner is now covering your backside. A non-committed poacher is like a politician that says one thing and does another: You don't trust them and you don't vote them in for a second term.

   An effective time to poach is after your partner has returned the serve to a weak opponent and you anticipate a feeble 3rd shot. A poach can also be spontaneous, especially if your partner is slightly behind you and a return is popped up on your forehand side.
g. Franchise player-When competing in major competitions and there is a discernibly better-skilled player (franchise player), it is possible to position the less skilled player on his/her strongest court side most if not all the time. For example, if a right handed franchise player is serving from the right side of the court (deuce court), his/her partner being a stronger forehand player (right-handed) will stand in the deuce court and to the right of the franchise player. After the serve the franchise player will move to the left court (add court) and take over that position leaving his/her partner in their strongest cover position.

   If the better-skilled partner is serving from the add court or his/her partner is serving from the deuce court, no adjusting or switching is necessary. However, if the weaker partner is serving from the add court, they need to switch after the serve.

   Partners must keep track of where they belong, since they are constantly switching sides. The first server for a team will always be in the deuce court when their team score is even and always be in the add court when their score is odd.
   Caution!

   If you think you are the franchise player and you're not, you may have a difficult time finding double partners to play with. Remember that no one likes to play second fiddle all the time, especially if they are watching the game 80% of the time. An overly aggressive doubles partner will often make as many or more unforced errors as his/her partner because they are attempting more difficult shots from more demanding positions.

   If you are playing with a long-term doubles partner (as in spouse partners), have patience and allow them to hit as many balls as possible. You will be surprised at how fast they will progress in their skill and how quickly their confidence will improve.

4. COMMUNICATION

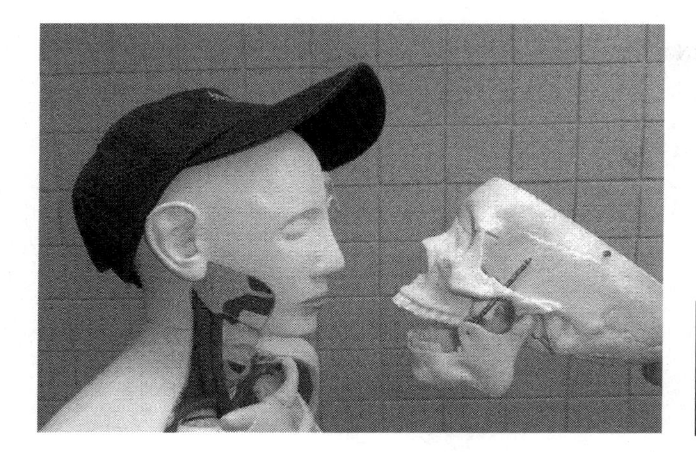

Death and life are in the power of the tongue: and they that love it shall reap the reward.

a. Talk with your partner before and during points. The following is a list of things you can talk about:
    i. Limitations and strengths of your opponents
    ii. Basic game strategies like covering for each other's disabilities, etc.
    iii. Who is going to cover the hallway (avenue) or the hits down the center court
    iv. On overhead shots yell "Mine", "Yours," but not both!
    v. When to poach
    vi. Words of encouragement…remember that positive reinforcement is the most effective kind of motivation!
    vii. Occasionally, you can tell a joke or point out how ugly your opponent's shorts are or if they'd look better without them. This is a good strategy if your partner is overly stressed out, but end with a comment to refocus on the next point like…"You'll do fine, just return the ball to the right side of the court."

Doubles Videos:

Video IV.1: Doubles Moving Together – 1.0 speed

Video IV.2: Doubles Strategy – Avenue – .50 speed

Video IV.3: Doubles Down the Line – 1.0 speed

Video IV.4: Double Switching Sides – 1.0 speed

Video IV.5: Doubles Cross-Over Coverage – 1.0 speed

BOOK V: MENTAL PREPARATION

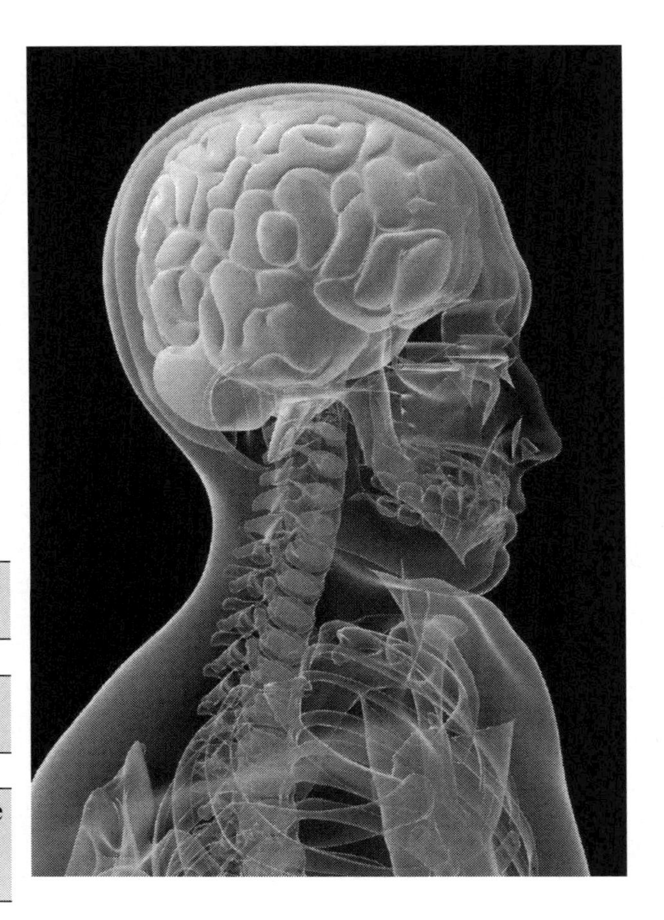

1. MENTAL PRACTICE AND IMAGERY

Overview: THERE IS NO SUCH THING AS MUSCLE MEMORY! Muscles are really quite dumb. They just try to respond to neurological impulses and commands sent from the central nervous system. Motor skill learning all starts upstairs in the penthouse suites. You've got to have something going on upstairs before anything happens downstairs. That almost sounds like a quote from a Kinsey Report. When the two connect, that's PURE MAGIC!

"Ninety percent of the game is half mental." –Yogi Berra (Hall of fame catcher for the NY Yankees

"The mind messes up more shots than the body." Tommy Bolt (Professional Golfer)

"The most important part of a player's body is above his shoulders." -Ty Cobb (Hall of Fame baseball player)

1.1 MENTAL PRACTICE

The practice of motor skills without overt movement can be accomplished by: 1. Mentally practicing skill strategies, focus cues, procedural aspects, or 2. Seeing and feeling actual skill performance (Mental Imagery). Most successful athletes incorporate some form of mental imagery and visualization into their physical practice to their advantage because it works. The brain cannot tell the difference between an actual physical event and one that is vividly imagined. Some studies have shown that mental practice has actually produced results similar to those found for physical practice and is always superior to no practice (Feltz & Landers, 1983 and Smith, Wright, & Cantwell, 2008).

Jack Nicklaus, one of the greatest golfer of all time, along with many other great athletes have commented on the use of imagery in preparing for competition.
"I never hit a shot, not even in practice, without having a very sharp, in-focus picture of it in my head. It's like a color movie." (Nicklaus, 1974, p. 79) How's your TV working?

1.2 INTERNAL & EXTERNAL PERSPECTIVES:

Athletes can visualize movements and performance from two different perspectives. The internal perspective is one in which the athlete imagines performing the activity from within his/her own body, feeling and using all the senses. This perspective is very natural for us, as it is how we actually view the world. In external imagery the performer sees himself/herself from outside the body watching from a distance, much the same way we would be viewing a video tape of the performance.

1.3 NOVICE AND HIGH PERFORMANCE ATHLETES

Both novice and expert athletes can benefit from mental imagery practice. However, for mental practice to be effective, a certain amount of skill is necessary. The most advanced players seem to benefit more than beginners. Regardless of the perspective, the most effective imagery is one in which the athlete can most closely replicate or simulate both the look, feel, sounds and smells of the actual performance. Perhaps this is why an experienced athlete may benefit more from mental imagery than a beginner: They can recall with more vivid details how a magical performance feels (Hardy, 1997 and Hardy & Callow, 1999). All mental practice sessions should only focus on successful skill execution. So, if you are incapacitated by illness, injury, or bad weather, that's no excuse for not practicing.

1.4 PAIVIO'S CONCEPTUAL MODEL OF IMAGERY (Paivio, 1985)

Why mental imagery practice? Specificity of purpose will help athletes focus on areas that need improvement and is closely related to the specificity principle of goal setting. Paivio's two-dimensional (cognitive and motivational) conceptual model of imagery identifies 5 different types or functions of mental imagery. Athletes should choose which function best meets their needs.

PAIVIO'S CONCEPTUAL MODEL OF IMAGERY

PRINCIPLE/FUNCTIONS OF MENTAL IMAGERY	DESCRIPTION/APPLICATION
1. Motivational Specific (MS)	The athlete pictures himself/herself in a specific highly motivating scenario. For example, visualizing hitting a short angle volley for the winning game point in pickleball, or bench pressing a new personal best.
2. Motivational General – Mastery (MGM)	The athlete imagines himself/herself in a general sports circumstance where he/she shows confidence and focus in a stressful situation. For example, an athlete may think, "I'm going to make this shot" or "I can win this game."
3. Motivational General – Arousal (MGA)	The athlete imagines a total ability to control feelings of anxiety. For example, he/she imagines taking slow deep breaths and feeling a wave of calmness and control.
4. Cognitive Specific (CS)	The image here is to visualize executing a perfect sport skill in competition. For example, hitting a backhand short-angle winner against a specific opponent in national competition.

5. Cognitive General (CG)	This function is visualizing individual or team strategies. For example, in pickleball imagining moving in tandem with your partner to cover wide dinks at the net.

7 PRINCIPLES AND APLLICATIONS OF MENTAL PRACTICE

THE 7 PRINCIPLES OF MENTAL PRACTICE	APPLICATIONS
1. Optimal Performance involves both physical and mental practice and utilizes both internal and external perspectives.	1a. Athletes should be taught to use mental practice in conjunction with physical practice. 1b. Mental imagery can be used by itself before practice or a game in the locker room, before retiring at night or when actual practice is not feasible. 1c. Athletes should use both internal and external imagery.
2. The more skillful athlete will realize greater benefits from mental practice than the novice.	2a. When learning a new skill, instructors should highlight the difference between a good and bad performance. 2b. Coaches should also ask the players how it felt when they performed well. 2c. Introduce mental practice after the student has the basic skills and understanding of the performance.
3. Motor skills that have large cognitive components (strategy, planning, decision making, cue identification etc.) may benefit more from mental practice.	3a. The greater the amount of cognitive processing in a skill, a greater amount of mental practice should be utilized. 3b. Mental imagery has two functions: cognitive and motivational. In simple tasks (e.g. weight training), the motivational aspect may be very valuable.
4. More is not necessarily better for mental practice.	4a. Attention and focus on details are essential for effective mental practice. Once mental fatigue sets in or attention fades, go on to something else. Focused repetition is more beneficial than duration. 4b. Typical sessions last about 5 to 15 minutes. Quality should be the main emphasis in mental practice. This is the same principle that is applied for plyometric training (a form or physical conditioning designed to increase muscular power).
5. Players can imagine movements from either an **external perspective** (like watching your performance on an instant video replay), or an **internal perspective** (the way you feel	5. In pickleball, you can watching yourself from an external perspective perform a perfect overhead smash, which may improve your form. Using an internal perspective will

and move when performing an action).	connect the action with the desired outcome, and produce additional benefits, so you may want to try both perspectives.
6. A simple multi-step program to develop imagery skill may be helpful (Vealey and Greenleaf, 2010).	A more formal program to improve imagery capability might include the follow steps: 6a. Choose a quiet place where you will not be disturbed. 6b. Assume a relaxed position and try to attain a calm and tranquil state of mind. 6c. Select a variety of sport images visualizing people within the scene. For example, a beautiful gym with people playing volleyball, basketball etc. Focus on sounds, color, smells and textures. 6d. Now imagine yourself in a specific sport setting like pickleball. First view the game as if you were watching others playing. Finally, project yourself into the game and imagine you are performing the skills flawlessly with perfect precision. You should be aware of how you are moving, the sound of the ball striking the paddle, the rotation of the ball, the position of your opponent's paddle when striking the ball, the position of your partner, etc. The more detail the better. 6e. End the session by breathing deeply, slowly open your eyes and adjust to your surroundings. Informal or rapid visualization can also be effective during competition (e.g. The quiet eye technique). Between points or during time-outs you can visualize your next stroke or sequence.
7. Mental imagery is a skill and can be improved with practice.	7a. Just like any other skill, mental imagery must be practiced and refined. The results will be magical! P.S. Don't punish your kids for day-dreaming…They are probably practicing metal imagery…Just be sure they are practicing the right stuff!

2. GOAL ORIENTATION

Overview: Goal orientation is different than goal setting; it is about achievement-motivation of an athlete and how he/she thinks about accomplishing a specific goal. There are two goal orientations described in research that attempt to explain how people view their own abilities: 1. Task goal orientation, and 2. Ego goal orientation. (Nicholls, 1989, Duda & Treassure, 2006).

2.1 TASK (MASTERY) GOAL ORIENTATION

2.1 TASK (MASTERY) GOAL ORIENTATION or task-referenced judgment involves comparing one's performance to his/her previous performance. If athletes can perform a task better today than yesterday, chances are that they will be motivated to continue to work for mastery of a skill even if they fail to win games. However, at some point people may become aware of the social consequences of losing and become more motivated by winning.

2.2 EGO (COMPETITIVE) GOAL ORIENTATION or norm-referenced judgment involves comparing one's performance to the performance of others. This individual's perceived capability and self-confidence is measured by how he/she compares to others. Athletes can be task and ego oriented at the same time. One is not exclusive of the other.

3. GOAL SETTING

Overview: One of the main contributions of goal setting is to motivate and energize individuals to become more productive and effective. Goals not only motivate athletes but forces them to learn new and better ways of completing a task. Long-term goal = Incorporating at least one idea or principle from this book into your play or practice every week for the next year. If you keep doing the same thing, you will keep getting the same results. Short-term goal = Practice one principle out of the Pickleball Bible tomorrow.

> **"Obstacles are what you see when you take your eyes off your goal."**
> -Jim Lefebvre (Major league baseball player for the LA Dodgers)

> **"You've got to be very careful if you don't know where you are going, because you might not get there."** -Yogi Berra

3.1 BASIC TYPES OF GOALS:

1. **Outcome goals** focus on results of performance and often involve a judgment or an assessment of how well you do compared to others (e.g. winning a match or medal). A problem with this type of goal is that you don't always have control over an outcome (e.g. you could perform your very best and still not come home with a medal).
2. **Performance goals** emphasize improving one's performance over a past performance (e.g. decrease the number of unforced errors in a game). There is a little more control over this type of goal, but it may be affected by the skill level of your opponent (your own statistics may be worse when playing a highly skilled opponent than a novice).
3. **Process goals** focus more on the mechanics and techniques of how you perform a particular skill (e.g. keeping the tip of the paddle above the wrist during a volley). Literature has shown that process goals are more effective in terms of improvements in anxiety management.

> **"I tell the kids, somebody's gotta win, somebody's gotta lose. Just don't fight about it. Just try to get better."** –Yogi Berra

3.2 IMPORTANT CHARACTERISTICS OF GOALS

The acronym SMART is helpful in remembering some of the important characteristics of goals (Weinberg & Gould, 1999).
Goals should be:

S	• Specific
M	• Measurable
A	• Action-oriented (Behavoral)
R	• Realistic
T	• Timely

The acronym works quite well, but I would add a few other important characteristics:

1. **Challenging** - If a goal is not somewhat challenging a player my lose motivation and become bored.
2. **Written** – A worthwhile goal is not something you want to forget, so write it down and review it often.
3. **Use a combination of goals** – Process goals along with outcome or performance goals or both can be more effective than a single type of goal.
4. **Team and individual goals** – Performance as well as outcome goals should be set for teams. Research has shown that this type of team goal setting will also improve performance of individual team members (Johnson, et al., 1997).
5. **Practice and competition goal** – Practice goals will be more narrowly focused on process or skill improvement type of goals but competition goals should not be neglected during practice.
6. **Use short-term goals** to achieve long-range goals.
7. **Internalize goals** by letting athletes participate in the goal setting process.
8. **Consider personalities –** When setting team goals coaches should be aware of differences in personalities (e.g. internal & external locus of control – How much an individual needs to feel in control).

PRINCIPLES AND APPLICATIONS GOAL SETTING

PRINCIPLE	APPLICATION
1. Using multiple types of goals is the best strategy for improving performance.	1a. Only using outcome goals is the least effect strategy. 1b. When outcome goals are combined with either process goals or with process and performance goals the strategy is effective. 1c. Coaches and athletes need to understand and incorporate all three type of goals.
2. Effective goal setting will improve an athlete's attentional focus, persistence, effort, and develop new learning methods.	2a. The goal setting characteristics as outline in this sections must be learned and implemented by instructors and students in order to optimize performance. 2b. Poor goal setting techniques can result in student/athlete frustration and discouragement.

"I'm a firm believer in goal setting. Step by step. I can't see any other way of accomplishing anything." –Michael Jordan (Hall of Fame basketball player)

4. SELF-CONFIDENCE

Overview: Self-confidence can be thought of as an absence of negative thoughts. It is also one of the most important aspects of intrinsic or self-motivation and is essential for high performance. An athlete may have a general feeling of confidence in his/her abilities but also needs to develop situation-specific self-confidence, which is a **belief** that they can successfully execute a specific action or skill.

"Whatever the mind of man can conceive and believe, it can achieve." –Napoleon Hill (American Author of *Think and Grow Rich*- 1937)

4.1 EARLY RESEARCH BY ALBERT BANDURA indicates that there are four main principles that seem to contribute to self-confidence and a motivated athlete: 1. Successful performance, 2. Vicarious experiences, 3. Verbal Persuasion, and 4. Emotional arousal (Bandura, 1977).

BANDURA'S ELEMENTS OF SELF-CONFIDENCE (Self-Efficacy)

PRINCIPLE	APPLICATION
1. An athlete must experience success in order to build self-confidence.	1a. An athlete should remember and replay in their mind's eye successful past performances. 1b. Coaches/instructors in practice can simplify tasks and skills to decrease the difficulty and ensure success (e.g. feed volleys that are slow and on a predetermined side).
2. Vicarious or observational learn is an effective way to enhance self-confidence and learn a new skill.	2a. "If someone else can do it, I can do it." A student needs to have a template or model to copy. This can be a video or demonstration by the instructor or other students. Because there is so much information in a video or demonstration, the coach needs to focus the athlete's attention on specific cues or movements. 2b. Observational learning seems to be more effective as skill level goes up, but less effective as age increases. Maybe this is why it's harder to teach old dogs new tricks.
3. Verbal persuasion or positive external feedback from coaches, parents, or peers can greatly improve one's belief in their capability to perform a skill.	3a. It is important to note that reinforcement or feedback can be verbal or simply facial expressions or body language. In either case, positive reinforcement produces greater

	improvements in learning than negative reinforcement or punishment. 3b. Caution: When positive verbal feedback is given too frequently, it may lose some of its reinforcing power. Coaches should use faded or intermittent feedback to maintain reinforcing effectiveness. 3c. Negative self-talk can have a devastating effect on athletes. When thoughts are verbalized they become much stronger. Self-talk and thoughts should always be positive. Simply saying, "I can do this" is a very powerful verbal persuasion technique! 3d. Every negative should be countered by 3 positives. Negative comments have a much more powerful influence on people than positive comments.
4. Emotional arousal is an important factor in preparing for practice.	4a. Formal learning situations can be intimidating or threatening to new players. This heightened level of anxiety may make the athletes overly cautious and prevent them from taking necessary risks to improve performance. Coaches need to inform students that taking risks to improve performance is a necessary process and that they won't be sent to bed without dinner if they fail! 4b. If players are not focused or are disinterested, coaches need to get the athlete's attention and explain why you are doing what you are practicing and that there will be consequences for not putting forth appropriate effort; like going to bed without dinner.

"Do not let what you cannot do interfere with what you can do." –John Wooden (UCLA Hall of Fame Coach)

4.2 CONFIDENCE VS ARROGANCE

I really like the comparison made by former BYU Head Women's Tennis coach Craig Manning in his book *The Fearless Mind* (Manning, 2009). Coach Manning makes the comment that confidence and arrogance are mutually exclusive, and that confidence is more closely related to assertiveness while arrogance is more a kin to aggressiveness.

Confidence is believing that you are good at what you do, and is not dependent on a comparison with someone else. Confident athletes will be motivated to work hard and improve the skills they already have. On the other hand, arrogance will put down others in order to elevate self. Arrogant thought will most likely lead to mediocrity.

"When you have confidence, you can have a lot of fun. And when you have fun, you can do amazing things." –Joe Namath (Hall of Fame quarterback)

"Your body cannot out-perform what your brain thinks it can accomplish. To a great extent, limits are self-imposed." –Dr. Rick Lambson (Collegiate athlete and university professor)

5. ATTENTION/CONCENTRATION

Overview: In sport, there are few things that are as important as paying attention and concentrating on relevant cues and the task at hand. Concepts such as "Being in the Zone" and "Choking" both have strong ties with attentional focus.

"Concentration and mental toughness are the margins of victory." -Bill Russell (Hall of Fame basketball player)

5.1 DIRECTING ATTENTION

Research suggest that human have the capacity to direct attention in two dimensions: 1. Direction of attention (internal or external) and 2. Width of focus (narrow or broad). Coaches can direct their athletes to any number of internal or external sources of information by using verbal cues such as "keep a firm wrist" (internal/proprioception) or "follow the ball to the paddle" (external/environmental conditions).

Terminology:

1. External focus: Attention given to the outcome of an action.
2. Internal focus: Attention associated with *proprioception* or the awareness of the body's moving parts.
3. Motor program: A set of motor commands that defines the general but essential details of a skilled action (e.g. which muscle are involved, the timing and duration of muscle contraction etc.).
4. Open skills: Skills executed in a relatively stable, unchanging environment.
5. Closed skills: Skills performed in a changing, unstable environment.

DIRECTING ATTENTION Principles and Applications

Principles	Application
1. Attentional control can be developed for specific sports and skills.	1a. Coaches can help athletes identify and practice relevant cues to focus on. For example, focus on the gap between players of your opposing doubles team.
2. Research indicates that highly skilled players perform best when their focus is upon external environmental cues. However, beginners or less skilled players may benefit from internal focus or proprioception as well (Castaneda & Gray, 2007).	2a. Coaches need to redirect the attentional focus of skilled players to external factors. The motor programs for these highly skilled athletes are already well established. Focusing on internal proprioception may interfere or disrupt the unconscious, automated smooth execution of the skill. This

	disruption in automatic processing is often called "paralysis by analysis." 2b. Internal focus may help beginners establish and refine their motor programs but their attention should change to more external cues as their skill level increases.
3. The type of skill determines the direction of attention.	3a. For closed skills (stable and predictable environments like swimming) an internal focus may be more helpful (e.g. Rotate the shoulders and torso on the arm strokes). 2b. For an open skill like pickleball where the environment is constantly changing an external focus may be more beneficial (e.g. If your opponent is coming to the net, hit a return at his/her feet).
4. High anxiety and arousal levels have a tendency to shift attentional focus from external to internal causing "paralysis by analysis." High arousal levels will also induce distractions (ask any teenage boy), cause more erratic eye movements, slow reaction time and cause the athlete to miss more relevant environmental cues (like dad sitting on the front porch with a shotgun).	4a. Bottom line…Control arousal levels. This can be done by practicing deep breathing techniques (not hard, fast and shallow), progressive relaxation and using positive visualization techniques. Also remember that some nervousness is very normal and is important for preparing the body for competition.
5. An external/broad focus may help to anticipate the actions of your opponent and decrease your reaction time.	5a. A study of experienced tennis players showed that by focusing on their opponents head, shoulder, trunk and hips during the tennis serve, they were able to anticipate and move significantly quicker than inexperienced players that focused more narrowly on the ball (Ward, Williams & Bennett, 2002). Expert athletes also extract different types of information from their opponent's movement patterns than novice athletes. This information often includes regularities in movement behavior that can be used to anticipate subsequent actions.

6. MENTAL TOUGHNESS

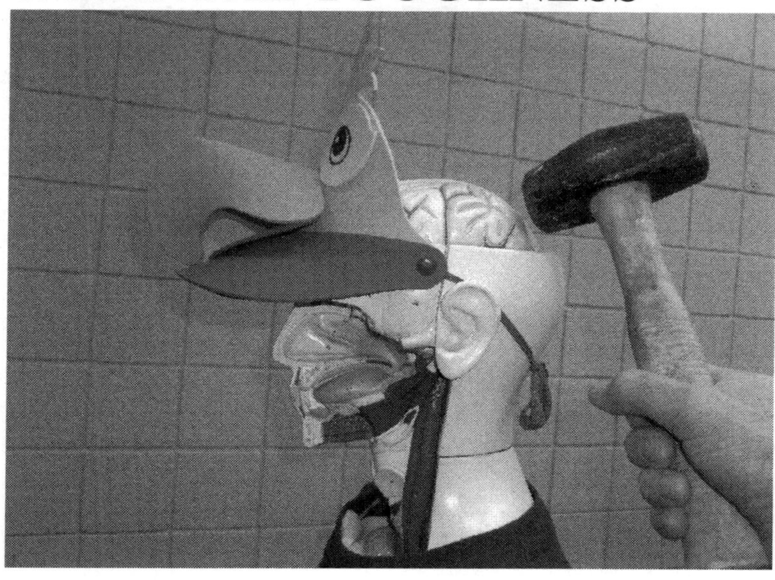

"The most important attribute a player must have is mental toughness." –Mia Hamm (National Soccer Hall of Fame inductee)

"Competitive toughness is an acquired skill and not an inherited gift." –Chris Evert (Hall of Fame tennis player)

"We gain strength, and courage, and confidence by each experience in which we really stop to look fear in the face... we must do that which we think we cannot." -Eleanor Roosevelt (Former First Lady)

Overview: Mental toughness is a difficult concept to define, but you know it when you see it. It seems to be the capability to remain determined, focused, confident and in control under the most stressful and pressure filled circumstances. There may be a natural ability associated mental toughness, but it can also be developed and augmented through proper mental training and practice.

The virtues that make up personal excellence are closely aligned with performance excellence and several researchers have suggested a need to integrate positive psychology and spirituality into mental skill training in order to achieve one's optimal potential (Watson & Nesti, 2005).

"You have to learn how to get comfortable with being uncomfortable." –Lou Piniella (Former major league baseball player and manager)

6.1 HOW IS MENTAL TOUGHNESS TRAINED?

Multiple research studies have found that psychological skills training (PST) based on goal setting, relaxation, imagery and positive self-talk were effective for improving sport performance (Weinberg & Williams, 2010).

Simplified PSI Training:

1. Practice and apply the principles outlined above in the first 5 concepts of MENTAL PREPARATION.
2. Practice the physical skills (target skill and target behavior) of pickleball. This will build your self-confidence.
3. Participate in tournaments, local competitions, lessons and other events (target context).
4. Focus on the steps leading to winning (process) rather than the end result (winning).
5. Be fearless and get out of your comfort zone by playing different people in different venues and competitions.

I have modified a great quote from Lou Holtz to make it more personal. Please forgive me Lou.

The original quote which is great for coaches and instructors:

"Leaders are obligated to bring out the best in their people. Most people will not reach their objectives unless you encourage them to take risks. You have to lead them out of their comfort zones. There is nothing more satisfying than knowing you have helped someone do the impossible. If you don't ask much form your team, you'll never scratch their potential (Holtz, 1998)." –Lou Holtz (College Football Hall of Fame Coach)

The revised quote:

"Individuals are obligated to bring out the best in themselves. You will not reach your objectives unless you take risks. You have to lead yourself out of your comfort zone. There is nothing more satisfying than knowing you have done the impossible. If you don't ask much from yourself, you'll never scratch your potential."

7. CHOKING

Overview: Choking, or a marked deterioration in execution of physical performance is a universal problem for all levels of competition, from novice to professional athletes. Literature clearly indicates that psychological pressure and stress have a debilitating effect on physical and cognitive (mental) performance. Choking under pressure is when a performer changes their normal routine or fails to adapt to environmental changes. This phenomenon affects athletes, musicians, dancers, broadcasters, actors, drivers and pilots. So, what is the cause and are there effective interventions to prevent or lessen the effects of choking?

"We all choke. Winners know how to handle choking better than losers." –John McEnroe

7.1 SHIFTING FROM AN EXTERNAL FOCUS OF ATTENTION TO AN INTERNAL FOCUS OF ATTENTION (BAD IDEA!)

Choking is a complex process that may involve interactions between attentional, emotional and cognitive factors. One thing that we can say is that in almost every situation, an external focus of attention is more effective for performance than an internal focus of attention (Wulf, 2007). See Section 5: Attention/Concentration for a refresher course on this topic.

So why did you fault on that critical serve, or hit that dink shot into the net on game point? Perhaps there was a shift from an unconscious (implicit) motor control process to a conscious (explicit) control process. Neuropsychologists believe that the implicit motor control mechanisms reside in the basal ganglia portion of the brain (This is not a reference to any other body part). This is the part of the brain that controls movement force and timing, which are critical in motor performance.

The cerebral cortex of the brain is activated when skilled athletes, who have achieved a high level of automatic processing, revert to a more conscious or explicit form of motor control, which often is awkward, slow-moving, and inaccurate. Remember that heightened anxiety has a tendency to shift attentional focus but the use of visualization on outcome results is an effective strategy in maintaining an external focus and becoming a "**clutch player**."

7.2 PARALYSIS BY ANALYSIS (ANOTHER BAD IDEA!)

In high-pressure situations an athlete may think too much and try to: 1. Control their movements in a conscious manner, 2. Remember too many procedural things, or 3. Focus on too many performance cues. There is a limited capacity for short-term memory, so try to keep it simple and attend to desired outcomes and the most important performance cues. Attentional capacity also narrows during stress, so by keeping it simple and relying on your own efficient motor programs, you will be able to recognize changes in the competitive environment.

7.3 THE IRONIC EFFECT

Story – Don't do that!

You're in the third set of a championship match and you are returning serve down 9-10. There is a slight breeze blowing directly behind you which has contributed to several of your returns going long past the baseline. Your mind now screams, "Don't hit it long!" Oops...Dang! Lost point, lost game, lost match!

Doing exactly what you don't want to do is a phenomenon that is referred to as the ironic effect (Beilock et al., 2001). Under normal conditions an athlete is able to replace negative thoughts with positive correct visions. However, when individuals are overwhelmed with anxiety and arousal levels are very high, the unconscious mind attends to the negative thoughts which control the unwanted action outcomes.

Strategies to overcome the ironic effect:

1. **Use attentional focus** (quiet eye strategy) to fixate on the intended target and the desired outcome.
2. **Change your thought pattern** from what I don't want to do, to "this is what I want and can do."
3. **Access your "Zone File"** and play one of your success videos. You can create a mental file for every sport or activity that you engage in. Every awesome shot, presentation or action should be saved and filed in your specific zone file and should be accessed and reviewed regularly, whether during competition or just daydreaming (see section 8.1 below).

"**When you have fun, it turns all the pressure into pleasure**." –Ken Griffey Jr. (All-Star baseball player)

"**Concentration is a fine antidote to anxiety.**" -Jack Nicklaus (Hall of Fame Golfer)

8. "THE ZONE" or "Unconscious Competence"

Overview: Achieving extraordinary, peak performance without conscious thought is an awesome magical experience. In reality, being in the zone should be thought of as the perfect marriage between mind and body. Even though it may seem that our brain is divorced from our physical movements, at some level the central nervous system is always in control. Far from not being involved, the brain is in a "do not interfere" mode and is running the optimal motor program for the given situation.

8.1 THE ZONE FILE is a simple yet powerful concept that has been effectively utilized by many athletes, presenters, teachers, musicians, and performing artists. It is simply remembering those awesome moments that resulted in exceptional performances. Here are a few suggestions for creating and using your file:

1. When those moments happen, take a few seconds and consciously tell yourself, "That was unbelievable. I'll put that in my pickleball volley file." Be careful not to dwell on the shot too long. You will need to focus on the next point.
2. After the match review in your mind the great plays and write them down in a journal. The more you interact with those experiences, the more permanent and accessible they will become in your long-term memory store.
3. These files can and probably should be a part of pre-game preparation and used during the contest, especially with anxiety build-up and when there is a break in action. These memories will work to build confidence and reduce arousal levels.
4. Eliminate the "screwed-up" shots by quickly telling yourself, "This is how I will do it next time." Then forget it and move on by focusing on the next shot.

8.2 CHARACTERISTICS OF A PHYSICAL GENIUS

A few years ago, Malcolm Gladwell (1990) wrote an article titled, *"The Physical Genius: What do Wayne Gretsky, Yo-Yo Ma, and brain surgeon named Charlie Wilson have in common?"* Within the article he identifies three important characteristics of a physical genius.

1. **Natural abilities** – These are the inherited traits that you were born with that include: multi-limb coordination, simple reaction time, manual dexterity, aiming, stamina and explosive strength to name a few (Fleishman, 1964).
2. **Practice** – One's capabilities are the athletic skills that are developed and perfected through countless hours of practice, training and mental preparation.
3. **Imagination** – This is what separates the physical genius from the really good athlete. It is the ability to generate multiple scenarios to win. The elite athlete will not be flustered or disturbed by different situations in a contest. There are no surprises only solutions.

Story - Wayne Gretsky

In a 1981 ice hockey game against St. Louis, Wayne Gretsky, with the puck and standing behind the opponent's goal, saw an opportunity for a scoring shot. In his mind he calculated angles and distances and then with great precision bounced the puck off the back of the goalie into the net. Now that's imagination!

Great athletes use their imaginations in particular and sophisticated ways. Great pickleball players develop the capability to anticipate where the ball is going and how to return it. They have either physically or mentally rehearsed every possible shot that they may face in competition and have visualized a perfect answer. When (not if) a great athlete makes a mistake, they have the imagination to replay what they had done and how they might have done it differently. They don't dwell on the mistake, they visualize the solution.

8.3 PERFORMANCE ROUTINES

Performance routines have been shown to be very effective in sports performance (Lidor & Mayan, 2005) and are probably an essential component of consistent execution and keeping oneself in the zone. There are three classifications of routines:

1. **Pre-performance routines** take place just prior to the initiation of a shot or action. This type of routine helps the athlete to focus upon external relevant stimuli and may be enhanced by a tactile component (e.g. call the score, bounce the ball twice, quiet eye routine, a deep breath and serve). A disruption in pre-performance routine may adversely affect performance of an athlete (Foster & Weigand, 2006).
2. **Between-play routines** take place during breaks in action and between points or change-overs. During this time a player may play a zone file, get a drink, focus on strategy or just engage in light conversation with a partner.
3. **Post-performance routines** take place immediately following a play or even a match. During this phase a player should clear his/her mind of any negative or poor play and focus on positive self-talk, and maybe pull out a zone file or two. After a poor match performance the player should counter-act any negative aspect of his/her play by pointing out 3 positive things that they accomplished.

Each routine is highly individualistic and depends on the game, the player's personality, superstitions, and coping resources and skills. Nevertheless, each routine should always take about the same amount of time. Some players have a tendency to either speed-up or slow-down play and routines when things get stressful. Be consistent in performance, routine actions and timing.

FINAL WORD

Every concept covered in this "Bible" will help you access "The Zone" and stay in it. The physical skills are important to master through intentional focused practice, but remember what Yogi said, **"Ninety percent of the game is half mental."**

P.S. If you have a great game, drill or fun activity associated with pickleball, send it to our website and you might be famous by Friday, or in our next edition of the PB Bible (We will give you full credit and maybe sent you a plate of cookies.)

For more information and instructional videos, please order the DVD:

The Pickleball Bible,

now available online.

VI. TALKING THE WALK GLOSSARY

Add Side: The right side of the court from where a singles player will always serve if his/her score is zero or even.

Adjustment Steps: The final quick steps to get the body in correct position before the final step into the ball.

Arrogance: Putting down others in order to elevate self. Arrogant thought will most likely lead to mediocrity.

Attention (Broad): Attention given to multiple elements of an action.

Attention (External): Attention given to the outcome of an action or environmental conditions.

Attention (Internal): Attention associated with *proprioception* or the awareness of the body's moving parts.

Attention (Narrow): Attention given to very specific elements of an action.

Avenue: The space between the two opposing players in doubles. This space is also known as the "hallway" and the "alley."

Backhand Sweep: A fast backhand return initiated by lifting the elbow.

Bowling Ball or Basic Serve: A serve technique in which a serve is executed with the tip of the paddle pointing straight down.

Choking: A marked deterioration in execution of a physical performance.

Cobra: An aggressive hit off the dink to the opponent's body.

Combination Drills: Drills that use different and multiple combinations of skills that are common during a contest.

Competent bystander: A player who feels incompetent and discouraged because of the difficulty of the drill or competition and will not try to engage in the activity, but will let others cover for him/her.

Deceleration: An absolutely terrible technique of trying to slow down the velocity of the paddle through a swing.

Deuce Side: The left side of the court from where a singles player will always serve if his/her score is an odd number.

Dink: A soft shot that is initiated close to the net and lands in the kitchen area.

Dominant Eye: The visual equivalent of handedness. Each individual has a dominant eye which controls many important visual functions, such as the ability to aim, and directing focus of attention. It also guides the other eye and directs attention and fixation on moving environmental objects.

Double Bounce Rule: The receiver must let the serve bounce once before the return and the serving side must let the return bounce once.

Drop Volley: A soft backspin volley landing in or near the kitchen.

Eight: A lucky number in China.

Fault: Any action that violates a rule and results in loss of serve or a point for the opponent.

Franchise Player: A highly skilled player, the one you want to avoid.

Goals (Outcome): A focus on the results of performance and often involve a judgment or an assessment of how well you do compared to others

Goals (Performance): Emphasizes improving one's performance over a past performance.

Goals (Process): A focus on the mechanics and techniques of how you perform a particular skill. Literature has shown that process goals are more effective in terms of improvements in anxiety management.

Grip (Hammer): A grip on the paddle where the thumb is on top of the first finger. Avoid this grip and you will be famous by Friday!

Grip (Hand Shake or Basic): A grip on the paddle where the "V" made by the first finger and thumb is placed on the top edge of the handle and the thumb is touching the second finger.
Half-Volley: A defensive shot where the ball bounces at your feet and is hit as it rises from the court.
IFP Rating System: The International Federation of Pickleball (IFP) has established 9 skill level ratings: 1.0, 1.5, 2.0, 2.5, 3.0, 3.5, 4.0, 4.5, and 5.0. The IFP Rating is primarily based on stroke proficiency and a players understanding and application of rules and strategies.
Ironic Effect: A phenomenon that one does exactly what they don't want to do.
King's/Queen's Court: Competition where winners will rotate toward a specified "King's Court," and the losers will rotate in the opposite direction. This will eventually even out the level of competition.
Lead-Up Games: Simplified versions or variations of a game.
Lob (Offensive): Is not as high as the defensive lob and can be hit with some top spin over the backhand side of the opponent. This shot is usually attempted after an exchange of dinks at the net.
Lob: A ball hit high enough to pass over the head of a net player or just a high arching serve or return.
Long Drop Shot: Usually the third shot in a rally in which the player attempt to drop the ball into the no volley zone from deep in his/her own court. Is one of the most important shots in doubles.
Mental Imagery: Seeing and feeling in one's mind an actual physical performance.
Mental Toughness: The capability to remain determined, focused, confident and in control under stress.
Midcourt or "No-man's Land": A position on the court between the baseline and the kitchen.
Muscle Memory: No such thing. Muscle are really dumb and only react to instructions from the central nervous system.
Negative Body Language: When a player shows slumping shoulders, head down, and knuckles dragging on the ground. This feeds your opponent with extra resolve to finish you off and put you out of your misery.
No Volley Line: The line seven feet from the net which defines the no volley zone. It is also referred to as the "short service line."
No Volley Zone: The area seven feet from the net where volleys are not permitted. It is a fault if a player or his/her paddle touches within the area or line of the kitchen on a volley or a follow through of a volley. This area is also known as the "Kitchen."
Paralysis by Analysis: Thinking too much and trying to control well-learned physical movements in a conscious manner.
Perspective (External): A performer sees himself/herself from outside the body watching from a distance, much the same way we would be viewing a video tape of the performance.
Perspective (Internal): An athlete imagines performing an activity from within his/her own body, feeling and using all the senses.
Poaching: A doubles strategy in which a player will cross-over to the partner's side to make a volley.
Pronation: Inward rotation of the forearm. A good technique for overheads.
Quiet Eye Technique: A technique in which uses a pre-execution period of visual fixation between 1-2 seconds. This really works, try it!
Segmentation: A technique of breaking down a skill into smaller segments and adding each segment together until the whole skill is completed.
Self-Confidence: The absence of negative thoughts or believing that you are good at what you do, and is not dependent on a comparison with someone else.
Specificity Principle: The best practice which most closely simulates the skills, movement patterns, and the environmental conditions of the actual contest.
Split-Stop: A technique when both feet land together and split apart at the same time in preparation of a return.
Supination: Outward rotation of the forearm.
Tail: A players buttocks.

Target (Primary): A target that you can hit confidently with a forehand stroke.

Target (Secondary): A target that you will go for if the serve forces you to hit a backhand, or pulls you into a stretched position. This shot might be a medium paced shot deep to the center of the court.

Target Behavior: The specific movements or cues that are essential in performing a skill.

Target Context: The conditions under which you want to perform the skill.

Target Skill: The skill you want to develop with practice.

Vision (Ambient or Peripheral): A vision system that involves both the central and peripheral portions of the visual field and is specialized for movement control. It detects position, speed and direction of objects outside of focal vision and contributes to fine motor movements without our conscious awareness.

Vision (Focal): A vision system that is used primarily to identify objects in the center of the visual field and contributes to our conscious perception of objects.

Volley: A shot hit out of the air before it bounces.

Wrist Extension: A position of the wrist which is opposite of flexion. Also referred to as "laying back the wrist." This is a fundamentally sound position for many pickleball strokes.

Zone, The: Achieving extraordinary, peak performance without conscious thought.

REFERENCES:

1. Abrahamsen, F. E., Roberts, G. C., & Pensgaard, A. M. (2008). Achievement goals and gender effects on multidimensional anxiety in national elite sport. *Psychology of Sport and Exercise*, 9, 494-464.
2. Bandura, A., (1977). Self-efficacy: Toward a unifying theory of behavioral change. *Psychological Review*. 84, 191-215.
3. Beilock, S. L., et al. (2001). "Don't Miss!" The debilitating effects of suppressive imagery on golf putting performance. *Journal of Sport and Exercise Psychology*, 23, 200-221.
4. Castaneda, b., & Gray, R. (2007). Effects of focus of attention on baseball batting performance in players of differing skill levels. *Journal of Sport & Exercise Psychology*, 29, 60-77.
5. Christina, R.W., & Alpenfels, E., (2002). Why does traditional training fail to optimize playing performance? In E. Thain (Ed.), Science and Golf IV: Proceedings of the World Scientific Congress of Golf (pp. 1-15. New York: Routledge.
6. Duda, J. L., & Treasure, D. C. (2006). Motivational processes and the facilitation of performance, persistence, and well-being in sport. In J.M. Williams (Ed.*), Applied sport psychology: Personal growth to peak performance* (pp. 57-81). New York: McGraw-Hill.
7. Feltz, D.L., & Landers, D.M., (1983). The effects of mental practice on motor skill learning and performance: A meta-analysis. *Journal of Sport Psychology*, 5, 1-8.
8. Fleishman, E.A. (1964). *The structure and measurement of physical fitness.* Englewood Cliffs, NJ: Prentice-Hall.
9. Foster, D. J. & Weigand, D. A. (2006). The effect of removing superstitious behavior and introducing a pre-performance routine on basketball free-throw performance. Journal of Applied sport Psychology, 18, 167-171.
10. Gladwell, M. (1999, August 2). The Physical genius. *The New Yorker*, 84-92.
11. Hardy, L. (1997). The Coleman Robert Griffith Address: three myth about sport psychology consultancy work. *Journal of Applied Sport Psychology*, 9, 277-294.
12. Hardy, L., & Callow, N. (1999). Efficacy of external and internal visual imagery perspectives for the enhancement of performance on tasks in which form is important. *Journal of Sport and Exercise Psychology*, 21, 95-112.
13. Henry, F.M. (1968) Specificity vs generality in learning motor skill. In R.C. Brown & G.S. Kenyon (Eds.), Classical studies on physical activity (pp. 331- 340). Englewood Cliffs, NJ: Prentice-Hall. (Original work published 1958)
14. Holtz, L. (1998). *Winning every day: The game plan for success* (p. 157). New York: HarperCollins Publishers, HarperBusiness.
15. Johnson, S. R., et al. (1997). The effects of group versus individual goal setting on bowling performance. *The Sport Psychologist*, 11, 190-200.
16. Lidor, R., & Mayan, Z., (2005) Can beginning learners benefit from preperformance routines when serving volleyball? The Sport Psychologist, 19, 343-363.
17. Manning, C. (2009). *The fearless mind 5 essential steps to higher performance*. Springville, UT: Cedar Fort, Inc.
18. Metzler, M. (1989). A review of research on time in sport pedagogy. *Journal of Teaching in Physical Education*, 8, 87-103.
19. Nicholls, J. G. (1989). *The competitive ethos and democratic education*. Cambridge, MA: Harvard University Press.
20. Nicklaus, J. (1974). Golf my way (p 79). New York, NY: Simon & Schuster.
21. Paivio, A. (1985). Cognitive and motivational functions of imagery in human performance. *Canadian Journal of Applied Sport Sciences*, 10, 225-285.

22. Silverman, S. (1985). Relationship of engagement and practice trials to student achievement. *Journal of Teaching in Physical Education*, 5, 13-21.
23. Smith, D., Wright, C.J., & Cantwell, C. (2008). Beating the bunker: The effect of PETTLEP imagery on golf bunker shot performance. *Research Quarterly for Exercise and Sport*, 79, 385-391.
24. Vealey, R. S., & Greenleaf, C. A. (2010). Seeing is believing: Understanding and using imagery in sport. In J. M. Williams (Ed.), *Applied sports psychology: Personal growth to peak performance* (pp. 267-304). Boston: McGraw-Hill.
25. Vickers, J.N. (1996) Visual Control when aiming at a far target. *Journal of Experimental Psychology*: Human Perception and Performance, 22, 342-354
26. Ward, P., Williams, A. M., & Bennett, S. J. (2002). Visual search and biological motion perception in tennis. *Research Quarterly for Exercise and Sport*, 73, 107-112.
27. Watson, N. J., & Nesti, M. (2005). The role of spirituality in sport psychology consulting: An analysis and integrative review of literature. *Journal of Applied sport Psychology*, 17 228-239.
28. Weinberg, R. S., & Gould, D. (1999). *Foundations of sport and exercise psychology*. Champaign, IL: Human Kinetics.
29. Wulf, g. (2007). Attention and motor skill learning. Champaign, IL: Human Kinetics.

StarryNightPublishing.com

Made in the USA
Coppell, TX
20 November 2020

41769353R00057